# MEN
## ON
# DivorcE

# MEN
## ON
# DivorcE

*Conversations with*
## DENISE WINN

PIATKUS

© 1986 Denise Winn

First published 1986
by Judy Piatkus (Publishers) Limited, London

British Library Cataloguing in Publication Data

Winn, Denise
  Men on divorce.
  1. Divorced men    2. Adjustment (Psychology)
  I. Title
  306.8'9      HQ814
  ISBN 0 86188 524 4


Designed by Sue Ryall

Phototypeset in 11/13pt Linotron Sabon by
Phoenix Photosetting, Chatham
Printed and bound in Great Britain by
Mackays of Chatham Ltd, Kent

# Contents

## Acknowledgements

My thanks and gratitude to all the men
who helped me create this book.

# Introduction

The experience and consequences of marriage breakdown affect men and women equally profoundly. Yet men tend to find it far less easy or acceptable than women to articulate their deepest feelings, particularly their worries, fears, insecurities and hurts. Sometimes men cannot admit them to themselves. They therefore find it harder than women to come to terms emotionally with what has happened to them, to their lives and to the people in their lives.

When a marriage goes wrong, men often have to flounder alone in emotional turmoil because they do not have the same support network of friends, male or female, that women traditionally have. Men usually claim that they find it easier to talk to a woman than to another man. Women are often more ready to listen and to understand. And that is one reason why I, rather than a man, was asked to write this book.

The book's aim is to share with men and with women the feelings of a substantial number of men who have been through the traumatic experience of divorce, and to show how they made sense of and survived it. For men who are finding it hard to come to terms with a failed marriage, or the prospect of one, I hope it may be helpful, in the way that we all so often gain insight or comfort from something other people say, whether or not their circumstances and experience are identical to our own. It may also help to see how very different people have found different solutions to the profound problems posed by marriage breakdown and subsequent living. Certainly those men I spoke to who did know someone close who had been through divorce said they derived significant support from sharing the experience.

To women, whatever their circumstances, I hope the book will show how much more similar than dissimilar to theirs are men's feelings about themselves, and their relationships with partners and children.

I did not want to write a casebook, nor an analysis of men, nor a practical guide to coping with divorce. (Of the latter, there are several excellent books available, a list of which can be obtained from the National Marriage Guidance Council.) I wanted instead to look in detail at the views and feelings of 26 divorced men. These men are quite various, in background and personality, though not necessarily typical of a cross-section of the population at large. They were randomly selected in so far as they responded to requests spread by word of mouth or via organisations, but they speak as individuals, not as representatives of any statistical norm. In fact, I was particularly struck by just how individual each story was and wonder, as a result, whether statistics are in any way significant on this sort of subject.

These men are aged from twenty-seven to sixty-seven, with the majority in their early forties. They came from various parts of Britain and Ireland. Some had left school at sixteen, others went on to university and entered professions. Among the men I met were a teacher, a lecturer, an artist, a writer, an architect, a designer, a scientist, a builder, a decorator, an engineer, several businessmen and one who was unemployed.

Their experience of marriage is also varied: some married young, others in their middle to late thirties; most had children, but not all; some split up from their wives when the children were very young, others when the children were in early or late teens; some have good relationships with their ex-wives, others don't; some have or had free access to their children, for others it was limited or non-existent, while a few had custody them-selves. About half of the men have re-married, five have divorced more than once and twelve are currently living alone. For some of the men divorce was very recent, others are looking back from many years on.

The men I spoke to are obviously also self-selected, in that they are the ones who were willing to talk to me. Probably about the same number of men were approached who were not prepared to speak. This may have been because their feelings of loss or resentment or guilt were too personal or because they felt their new wives would feel uncomfortable, or because they felt suspicious about who I might be. Those who did talk to me were generous and courageous to do so, because they hoped that sharing their feelings might be of help to others. Many said that they wished that there had been something similar available for them to read when they were going through divorce. But talking so personally about themselves was something no one found easy, and some found very hard. I did notice, however, that those who had sought some kind of counselling or therapy during or after their marriage breakdown were more comfortable in this territory and keen to stress how important and liberating therapy had been for them in this respect. A number of men mentioned that the unusual experience of documenting their divorce and all that had gone before and after it had made them think about events and feelings in a way that they had not consciously done before, and that they had gained some insights.

I certainly believe that every man tried to be as honest with me as he could, but that doesn't mean that some areas of pain or guilt were not passed over, if too difficult to confront again or too threatening to reveal. Only one man felt extremely bitter towards his ex-wife, and admitted it. But no one used the time to put down former partners or attempt to show themselves in falsely favourable lights. On the contrary, a good few, it seemed to me, took more than their likely share of responsibility, through feelings of guilt and failure.

As the aim is to highlight how different people responded to or coped with different aspects of marriage breakdown, divorce and life thereafter, no stories are related in full in any one place but are followed through, where relevant, in consecutive chapters which chart the sequence of events and themes in chronological order.

The book begins by looking at the circumstances in which the men married. I thought it important to go back that far because so many mentioned the effects they felt their childhood and upbringing had on making them the people they have become and choosing the marriages they made. Of course countless people whose marriages are still content could no doubt cite similar beginnings to many of those featured in the following pages. The intention is not to suggest that people from particular backgrounds haven't a hope of a lasting relationship, but rather to share the understanding some men have gained which has reconciled them to their past behaviour and given them greater control over their choices in the future.

Similarly, childhood crops up repeatedly when a number of men talk about why they feel their marriages went wrong. It is striking that their feelings of failure to understand or communicate their feelings are so often attributed to upbringing. For many men, these were some of the most painful realisations to come to, and to learn to deal with.

I have included a chapter on the effects of affairs on men, their own or their wives', because so often affairs precipitated marriage breakdown, although they were not the cause, and had effects on later adjustment to relationships with ex-wives and to new relationships.

The chapter on break-up looks at the men's immediate responses to being alone (none of the men I interviewed went directly to live with another woman), whereas reactions to separation from children, or caring for children are dealt with more fully later on.

A number of men did seek some kind of therapy during or after their marriage breakdown and they explore the value of this. For many, it was a revelatory experience. The self-knowledge derived from counselling made them feel easier about talking to me in the first place. It is very likely that a great many men, and women, suffer more immediate bitterness over actual divorce settlements and arrangements for children than most of the men I spoke to expressed to me. Counselling may have helped here, but also time is the great healer, so that for these men emotions have become less charged and fraught circumstances have changed. In this respect certainly it is possible to be optimistic.

Finally, we looked at life after divorce and how the men have fared in relationships since. Again, experiences and reactions are wide-ranging, as are the criteria for fulfilment and contentment.

I should like to make it clear at this point that the men I met and interviewed on the whole gave the impression of being likeable and fun, or confident, strong, successful or attractive. Lively personalities or gentleness or wit or warmth or a sense of inner strength variously came across to me. Yet what they say in this book makes them appear very vulnerable or may make them seem weak and insecure. What I respect is that they were willing to show the kind of hurts nursed from childhood, to reveal the child still within – within all of us – which is never normally exposed to anyone who isn't very close. They show the feelings and fears which women are traditionally more prepared to acknowledge, but which most men feel obliged to hide and deny.

Not included, of course, are the wives' sides of the stories and I feel that, for this purpose, that is a strength. We are not here sidetracked into making irrelevant judgments about who was right and who was wrong, or who has suffered more. The book isn't about rights and wrongs, but about male perspectives on relationships. Our actions are, after all, guided by how we see things and not necessarily by how they actually are.

Having said that, I am particularly conscious that I, who drew together all the strands of what was said, who directed the presentation of these men's stories, am a woman. So I have made every effort not to make personal or sex-biased judgments. Any speculations or connections I have made are, I hope, clearly signposted as my own, while any conclusions that are reached are largely those of the men. For that reason, too, there is not only little comment from me in the main body of the book, but little generalisation drawn from the words or books of 'experts'.

However, a number of points that were made on various issues certainly gave me much food for thought and I have tried to address these in my 'Reflections' at the end, where it feels more appropriate to widen the scope and include what we know from surveys or psychology. I have also tried to look more generally at some of what has been said and written about the differences – and similarities – in the ways men and women feel and behave.

I have refrained from all but a few statistics and also from setting many people in the context of where they live, partly to protect their anonymity (all the names are fictional), and partly because I interviewed far too few to infer whether people from one part of the country, or another, are more likely to do or feel such and such or not. I also thought that, in the context of these relationships, the emotional climate of the childhood home was more important an influence than geography.

Similarly, I believe that it is the emotional climate of a marriage that dictates what happens within it. It is the needs and fears we bring to a relationship which, if not supplied or overcome, respectively, lead to marriage difficulties: needs and fears are fairly fundamental, however diverse the forms that the difficulties take. If a number of possible life scenarios are not included among the stories told in this book (no one was unemployed prior to their marriage collapse, for instance), that may only mean that the specifics differ, rather than the sources of the conflict. All too often we look outside of ourselves to explain dissatisfaction and while one couple may identify disagreement over the children as the problem and another may identify it as money, the underlying conflict may well be the same.

It seems to me, therefore, that the feelings expressed here are sufficiently universal to speak to everyone on some level. I know that, even though I am not actually married nor a man, I identified or empathised with much that I heard, and I have now, I hope, more understanding to bring to the relationship with the man in my own life. I certainly feel that men and women's feelings are much more similar than dissimilar, deep down, and it is mainly their expression or lack of expression of them that differs.

I hope the message of this book is positive, despite the fact that divorce is inevitably very sad. One in three married couples now gets divorced and who knows what percentage of the other two thirds is happy in their marriages. This book, by showing how some marriages went wrong, also lights the way towards putting others right before they break down. The lessons are as important for women as for men: we need to know ourselves before we can know someone else and be prepared to explore together.

# 1
# Why marriage?

Why does anyone marry? 'We were in love', 'I would have leapt mountains for her', 'we seemed so well-suited', 'she was so exciting/passionate/interesting/fun'. But heady passion and an ensuing deeper attachment are only part of what may prompt two people to commit themselves to each other, ostensibly for life, especially now that it is no longer taboo to leave it illegal.

A vast number of people marry when they are comparatively young, when life ahead is still an exciting adventure. They may be full of ideals about what marriage means, keen to change the pattern of their life so far or step a stage further into adulthood and responsibility. But they may have less understanding than they care to imagine about who they are as people, why they are as they are, what real needs they are looking to fulfil in marriage or the expectations they bring with them.

Men who are divorced are possibly more ready than most to dare to look below the romantic feelings and find what other forces were at work in propelling them towards the altar. They have usually spent a lot of time analysing what went wrong and some may have resorted, at some point en route between then and now, to professional counselling which helped them make more sense of the part their upbringing played in forming their attitudes towards marriage, and their behaviour within it.

Many of the men I spoke to said that they were now aware of the powerful, if passive part that upbringing and social pressures, as well as love, played in leading them towards the marriages they'd made, and the expectations they brought with them. But they had not been aware at the time of being anything other than self-directing. In fact, most marked for many, was an inability to express or identify the more vulnerable feelings and needs which motivated them into marriage as young adults. Feelings of hurt, insecurity and cravings for affection as well as dependency needs had been repressed, culturally unacceptable in males and therefore emotionally threatening and unpalatable. Many, looking back, felt they had been ill-equipped to manage the emotional minefield of marriage and that, had they been able to identify and deal with such difficulties earlier, their marriages might have had a better chance.

Laurie believes that suppression of his feelings as a child had much to do with the marriage he later chose. A warm, good-looking man, now in his forties, he has a quiet confidence which belies the struggle he had in coming to terms with himself and his past, a struggle which encompassed two failed marriages. He came from a small town in Ireland and was still living with his parents and working in a small insurance firm when he met his first wife at twenty-nine. He married her within six months of his mother's sudden death.

Life had not been particularly happy or successful for him up to that point. He had wanted to be a lawyer but, as he had failed crucial exams, his rather authoritarian father insisted he left school and took a job as an interim measure until he had decided what he really had the ability and application to do. The interim measure ended up lasting twelve years. Laurie, introverted and unconfident then, seemed to take it as his lot that he was stuck in an office and also stuck at home.

'My mother was always very over-protective of me. From an early age I was labelled the good boy and my elder brother the bad boy and I think we found ourselves acting out those roles. My brother left home quite young and didn't stay in touch and that made my mother rather more dependent on me. My mother was never a very well woman. It seemed to be expected that I'd stay at home and I felt I had to be around because my brother wasn't,' he said.

He earned very little at his job. When he was twenty-one he had wanted to marry but his parents – and hers – impressed upon him how poorly financially equipped he was to do so. He bowed to pressure and let the relationship go and in doing so, he feels now, he learned to suppress the more passionate side of his nature.

He met Carol, his future wife, because she lived nearby. 'A friend engineered a meeting,' he said. 'We enjoyed each other's company but were not deeply romantically involved. Then my mother died suddenly. Carol came to the funeral and afterwards we started seeing each other very regularly. I proposed to her within two months of my mother's death and she said that if I hadn't asked her, she would have asked me.

'I thought I was in love. With hindsight I can see that I was deluding myself. My upbringing had been so emotionally sheltered and my mother's death was an appalling shock to me. Nothing like that had ever happened to me and I wasn't prepared for it. I wanted to leave home and, because I had inherited money, I could afford to,' he said. Because he and Carol were good companions and shared similar interests, it seemed sufficient basis for marriage – at the time.

Only since has he realised that, in marrying so soon after his mother's death, he was trying to replace the loss of an important female figure in his life, and that his marriage was doomed to remain superficial because he had learned to suppress his own wants and deeper feelings.

Like Laurie, Neal also feels that an undue emphasis on duty and right behaviour in his upbringing led to his growing up without any real understanding of his own personality. He is an artist, very articulate and lively and very willing to make fun at his own expense. He is, by his own account, an extremely different person from the one who, twelve years ago, at the age of twenty-eight, met the girl he married:

'I met her because I wanted to marry. I was determined to marry. If it hadn't been her, it would have been someone else. I went on holiday and said to the friend I was with, "I'm going to meet my wife here." I had this idea I was ready to marry, I needed to marry. But if someone needs it like that, well, that's neurotic, isn't it!'

He duly met a 'doll-like vision' on his holiday and they quickly became engaged. Then he discovered that the woman he had become infatuated with as a fragile beauty was in fact anorexic. 'At that time, anorexia was a mysterious disease. All I knew was that she didn't eat and that making love to her was physically painful. My sympathy with her was mixed with abhorrence and then I felt guilt. I couldn't turn away from her just because I didn't fancy her, I felt.

'I can see now how my dutiful behaviour as a son, unquestioningly accepting authority of parent or teacher led me to be so naive at twenty-eight. I was a good Catholic, brainwashed into sacrifice. I was also very timid, so that accorded well with my instinct to be obedient.'

Their engagement had been announced within a month of their first euphoric meeting and by the time Neal discovered that the relationship lacked any real warmth on either side, he felt he couldn't back out. 'The whole machinery of the banns had got going and once the buttons are pushed, you are whisked off your feet', he said wryly. 'Families meet and swear instant friendship, the wedding gets planned and the invites go out to the cousins and the aunts. I felt I was putting everyone to such trouble by getting married in the first place. I could hardly have embarrassed them by not doing it after all – although of course they would have coped!'

He does think, however, that more than bad fate was behind both his and his wife's respective choice of partner. 'For my part I had fallen in love with a pre-pubescent child. But I was probably incapable then of relating to a fully developed physical woman, because I was not fully developed emotionally as a man.'

Neal's is perhaps an extreme case but, as he points out himself, emotional development has nothing to do with chronological age. Yet it is chronological age which is usually referred to when we consider it is 'time' to get married. Philip, at twenty-five, thought it was time. He was positively looking to get married because he needed to conform, for his own sense of identity, to what he saw as the norm. He fell prey to gentle family pressure.

'My father came from a broken home and was very anxious to see us happily settled down. Both my brother and sister had married,' he said. Philip, now forty-three, gives the impression of being a very urbane and witty, gentle and sensitive man but it has taken him a long time to overcome what he saw as his late sexual development, and the consequent sense of inadequacy which pervaded his first marriage.

He had been to a boys' boarding school because his mother had been very ill when he was a child, and at eighteen, when he went to university, was still very shy, unable to show affection easily and had 'no idea how to form relationships with girls or any adults'. He was attracted to girls but they were not attracted to him because he certainly didn't know how to charm, and was rather bookish and reclusive.

'I was still a virgin at twenty-three and very sexually frustrated. When I went back to college the following year, I thought in my subconscious that if I met no one this time, I wasn't normal. It does prey on your mind if you think you are the odd one out,' he said. 'So when I did meet and become extremely fond of a girl at college, I asked her to marry me. But I was awfully emotionally immature and needed much more experience of women.

'I had never been able to talk to anyone on an emotional level until I saw a psychiatrist when things were going wrong and unburdened myself completely. The inability to express myself was lifted.

'I had been unable to talk to my parents about anything except mundane things and all my feelings till that point had been self doubts. I couldn't have answered if my wife had said, "Do you love me?" I probably would have said, "What is love?" '

Laurie, Neal and Philip all came from stable homes with loving parents. But in none of their homes was there much open show of emotion. Men who came from similar backgrounds found that they went into their own marriage somewhat blindly, expecting it to work because that was their experience of their parents' marriages. They often married young, mistakenly believing marriage to be easier than it usually is.

'I got married at twenty-two,' said Steve. 'Why? I met someone I thought I wanted to be with exclusively for the rest of my life. I have the same ideals now, at thirty-four, about relationships as I did at fifteen, so my age has nothing to do with why it didn't work.' He saw his parents as happily married, his brothers had married and, as far as he was concerned, marriage was what followed when you fell in love and it worked. 'I had never met people who were divorced or had affairs. They were all storybook people to me,' he said. He had made an exclusive commitment and meant it, and the marriage broke up when his wife did have an affair. Despite the fact that he works in the film industry, hardly sheltered from the reality of ruined relationships, he remains bemused by it all.

As another man put it, referring to his homelife, 'I was brought up in cotton wool.' His parents presented a united front. They didn't argue in front of him and his brothers and didn't display any extremes of emotion, positive or negative. He feels it has taken him a long time, and two failed marriages, to acknowledge the full gamut of his own and others' feelings.

Conversely, for a couple of men it was the virtual lack of any real home life as children that made them too ready to find a replacement in marriage for the home they had never had. Dan, now in his late sixties, very strong, solid and quick to laugh at himself, married for the first time when he was twenty years old.

'We met at a dance. She was very pretty and seemed to like me too. We both wanted to get away from home, it was as simple as that.' His mother had been widowed at the end of the First World War, having only been married a year and seemed to harbour a bitterness against men, including the son who was going to grow up to be one.

Dan was often farmed out to stay with relatives because she didn't want him in the house and, when he was at home, he was never allowed to eat at the same table as his mother and his sister. He received no encouragement at school, no interest in his work and future, and became hardened early on against the harsh realities of his life. He made the only kind of marriage he knew existed, a practical marriage, which had little to do with real love and affection, neither of which he knew existed at all.

Sad-eyed Robert, a thirty-seven-year-old builder, was also looking for a home. 'I'm a firm believer that what happens later in life is a result of your childhood,' he said. His father had died when he was a child and, because their house had been tied to his job, Robert's mother and her five children ended up sharing his uncle's very small home. The children were variously sent off to boarding school because of the lack of space. Robert didn't adapt well and kept running away but when, at the age of eleven, he returned to live at home, he found himself living in fear of his uncle, who was very strict.

'I was so scared of him that sometimes I used to sleep in my sisters' room rather than pass his door to get to mine. He never allowed us to have friends home and we weren't too often allowed out,' he recalled. At fifteen he joined the army to escape. 'I enjoyed it. But I felt I'd had enough of discipline already, and so bought myself out at eighteen.' He stayed in the town where he had been in barracks, got a job as a labourer and started to build up a social life, with mates at the pub.

'But the trap I fell into was that I hadn't had a homelife before, so I wanted to settle down. I was nineteen when I met my wife. We were very attracted to each other, so we married a year later and took a small rented flat. I felt so happy. At long last I had a place of my own. And when we got rehoused by the council after our baby was born, to me the house was a palace, even though there was no bathroom and no heating. My wife didn't feel quite the same way.'

But while it was the gap left by a cold and distant homelife that motivated Dan and Robert towards marriage too early, coming from a too caring and, to him, too claustrophobic family was what spurred Tony to want to escape. Although born in London, he came from a close-knit Italian family who tended to stay within an Italian circle of relatives and friends. 'The pressure was enormous to stay within the family,' he said. 'They wanted me to marry an Italian girl, work in the family business and generally behave as my older cousins had done.

'But I had started college and was getting a taste for English culture. I met my wife when I was twenty and we married when I was twenty-three. She was my second girlfriend and I was definitely in love. But in marrying her then, when I hadn't had much experience of life, I was ensuring that I could cut my family ties and start to run my life my own way.'

Ben, a large gentle bear of a man, felt he was partly looking for a security he hadn't known he'd lost when he started living with Gail at the age of twenty-four and then married her two years later, due to subtle pressure from parents to legalise the alliance. Both his parents and Gail's had had acrimonious divorces.

'I was in my late teens when my parents separated and I was certainly upset, even though it wasn't a shock as I had seen them fighting for many years. The split-up came at a time when I was still going through my own adolescent rebellion, and it was also the '60s, with all the flavour of drugs and cults and everything changing.

'Everything in my life seemed chaotic all at once. I felt cynical and distrustful of relationships but I didn't realise how insecure I was, and I'm sure that the need for some stability and security was, on a primitive level, what motivated me to live with Gail.

'She struck me as very beautiful, blonde, fresh and confident. I was very confused and fragile, although she thought I was confident too. Because we both distrusted relationships, because of our parents, we behaved as if living together and then marrying was an experiment, a bit of a joke. The immediate force behind it was probably comfort: playing house, cuddles,sex; shared activities were just easier if you were married. It was also a drug or a red herring because, once you go into that comfort zone, playing house, you don't have to think about yourself so much. If you get into it quite young, there's a sort of symbiosis that blocks real discovery of self. We didn't know ourselves emotionally at all,' he says, eighteen years on.

A need for security, on one partner's part or both, was often what came to clinch the decision to marry. Though it is women who are more often construed as keen to 'get their man', through an inflated fear of being left on the shelf, there is it seems, often an answering echo in men's hearts. Contrary to feeling the world was their oyster, however independent, successful or attractive they were, many felt an urge to act on what options they already had.

Jeff, a suave and successful architect, married Kay when he was twenty-seven and had already known her some years. 'She was physically attractive, mentally stimulating and we could spend a lot of time together without feeling uncomfortable. She wanted to marry and after a while I began to wonder what I was holding out for. I thought I was in love and I knew I hadn't met anyone more interesting. Perhaps I wouldn't.

'I did feel I'd been cornered into marriage before I was ready but I didn't want to risk losing her,' he said.

Angus married actress Claire at twenty-five. 'Why did we marry? It was sort of panic. Twenty-five already! I'm on the shelf! A lot of my friends were engaged to be married. I liked her sparkly personality and she had a nice bum. We had interests in common and I thought, strictly pragmatically, am I likely to find anyone else? There was no blinding flash of realisation, we just drifted into it in the end.'

He thinks now that he was also attracted by Claire's, to him, unconventional homelife. He saw her parents as extremely emotionally out-going and warm. His own parents had been very conservative and undemonstrative and he himself had reached his 20s lacking self esteem or any real sense of identity. He was a systems analyst, bored in his job and felt his life was going nowhere.

'I hadn't developed as a person enough myself and I felt Claire gave me identity. I probably got married to break the pattern of my existence. I was dissatisfied with my life and, though I would have said then we were in love, I don't know if we were. We enjoyed each other's company and I loved being part of her warm, open family, but that probably isn't enough to marry for.

'Still, we did have a good time at first and, if I did get married to break out of a humdrum existence, it certainly worked on that score. She was very talented and full of mad ideas. She was adored by her family and put on a pedestal, led to believe that anything she wanted she could have. I did realise at the start, before we married, that she probably didn't have the tools to survive ordinary living but, being a chappy chap, I stuck it through. I probably hadn't got the tools to survive then either.'

For some the search for security took the form of a whirlwind marriage on the rebound after a previous failed relationship. One man said: 'I met my wife-to-be and something just seemed to click. We were engaged within six weeks and married within three months. It was only years later, in analysis, I discovered how strongly I had felt that the girlfriend I had had before, and who had left me, had been the right one for me and that I subconsciously nursed the belief that I should have been with her.'

Security to some others meant success and part of success was having a wife and children. When Pete met Pam, he was sixteen and working as a teaboy in an office, but rapidly on the rise to office junior, salesman and then stock control supervisor of a warehouse. He had big aspirations. 'Success to me was being good-looking, healthy, having a lovely wife, two kids, a car and my own house.

'I met Pam at a youth club. She was very attractive, long blonde hair – quite a catch. It looked good to be seen with her, we both looked good as a couple. We argued an awful lot and she was always threatening a break-up, which I didn't want. I continually chased her until I coerced her into marrying me.

'I was eighteen when I got engaged, she was seventeen. It didn't seem young to me because I'd had a lot of girlfriends and thought I'd been around. I was a man of the world by then, in *my* mind.

'I was twenty when we married and, a year later, Pam had a baby. I was in the electronics industry by then and working all the overtime I could.

Six months later we got our own house and almost a 100 per cent mortgage. But I was so proud. I thought to myself, "I'm on the right road now. One child and a house."

'It was all about the outward signs of success. I didn't know there was any other way to live.'

Some men married earlier than they might have planned because their girlfriends got pregnant. But to Joe, a cheerful, easy-going lab technician, it wasn't a catastrophe when he found himself married at the age of nineteen, and expecting to be a father shortly afterwards. 'We would have married anyway,' he said. He, like Pete, became happily immersed in the struggle for success, taking on two extra jobs to raise enough money for a mortgage. 'I didn't think I had missed out on life at all,' he recalled. 'Age wasn't the reason it went wrong.'

But if others did think, in retrospect, that they had married too young, several of those who left it till later did not automatically feel mellowed by maturity or more confident about their commitment. Very often it was a fear of repeating their parents' mistakes or of being tied down which had kept them single so long. Certainly Charles, now sixty and who didn't marry till he was thirty-eight, doesn't feel that he knew himself any better or had resolved any more of his personal problems than when he was twenty years younger. 'I hadn't even contemplated marrying earlier and all my energy was going into building up my business. I only married at all because my wife was so keen on marrying me.

'I was nervous of marriage. My hesitancy came from the fact that my parents had divorced when I was eighteen and I didn't want to make the same mistakes.

'Although I definitely had fears about being tied down, I was very pleased to have someone to run the home and produce children while I carried on my career. I just didn't think about the psychological side of it, her needs or mine. We had the same backgrounds in common but that was about all. I never even thought about whether I was sexually attracted to her. I really didn't know anything much at all,' he said.

Expediency and social pressures played a part in some other decisions to make things legal and perhaps served to deflect attention from the enormity of the step. 'I was going to America for work and she couldn't have come with me otherwise,' said Jay, now a deputy headmaster, who married his twenty-one-year-old wife when he was thirty. 'Also, her parents didn't approve of "sin" and when we stayed with them, we wanted to be able to sleep in the same bedroom. The big attraction between us was intellectual. She was very striking too but I just hadn't met anyone with whom I buzzed like that. We just talked and talked about ideas.'

'Why did we marry?' said Morris. 'We were twenty-two, we had been living together and it seemed a good idea at the time. It was partly parental pressure and partly boring practical reasons. We fancied ourselves as terribly outrageous but we weren't prepared to be as outrageous as we thought, in 1958. We drifted into our marriage.'

Drifting into it because it seemed the thing to do for one reason or another appeared to have an inexorable force even for men who claim they had low hopes of the marriage's chances from the outset. 'We had had the same sort of backgrounds, it just sort of happened,' shrugged matter-of-fact printer Malcolm twenty-five years on. 'Our friends were getting married and we got on reasonably well. I probably thought I was in love. But I was pessimistic from the start and I think my wife suspected it,' he said.

It is no doubt easier, when marriage has gone wrong, to remember one's misgivings at the outset – misgivings and doubts which are probably there even for those who make successful and lasting marriages. But some men did express these particularly strongly. Lawyer Lew, warm and charming and self-admittedly emotionally defensive, says he knew he was making a mistake. 'I was thirty-one and Judy and I had been living together for two years. I knew that Judy, in her heart of hearts, wanted to marry and I knew that I, in my heart of hearts, did not. I didn't think it was a good idea – her or marriage, although I must have loved her. I suppose living together felt safer because you could get out.

'I'd been innoculated against marriage since childhood. My parents had had a really boring marriage, as I saw it. They were both very timid souls. I was terrified that I would find my marriage boring too. I obviously didn't go into it wholeheartedly even when I capitulated. I developed an awful backache, two days before the wedding, which persisted for several months. It didn't seem a very good omen and we were both aware of that, but we soldiered bravely on for some years.'

Why marry when the doubts seem so strong? Perhaps because the doubts about not marrying seem equally forceful. When marriage is the cultural norm and a partner, whom one loves, is pressuring for marriage, it may be just as frightening to pass up the prospect of a life with that person because of what might be beginner's nerves. It may take just as much courage and self-knowledge to opt out as to opt in.

Donald, now forty, certainly had reservations. 'I was brought up in the pattern of thinking that the done thing was to marry and settle down. My brothers had married and they were younger than I was. But I had spent my childhood battling with my mother for independence and I wasn't going to give up my freedom lightly.

'Women I met at university all seemed to be looking for security, however self-sufficient they appeared, and thought that any problems between us would be solved if they had it. I didn't. When I met the woman I did marry, at twenty-nine, I was very attracted to her and decided, perhaps she was right, perhaps whatever problems we had would go away after all. Everyone else was getting married and I suppose I saw it as another new experience to explore, although that does sound a terribly negative approach.'

Inevitably, in retrospect, with a failed marriage stretching between then and now, the wedding bells start to seem more tawdry and tinny than they did. But most men could recall, with feeling, the strong love and attraction they had once felt towards their former wives. Their criticisms were of themselves, for embarking on marriage emotionally ill-prepared and seeking within it solutions which would not be found there, while also acknowledging the fact that they had lacked the emotional tools to tackle things differently.

'If only they had taught us in school about relationships and marriage,' growled one man, a sentiment that was echoed several times over.

# 2
# What went wrong?

'Any regrets? What's the point?' shrugged one man, looking back at the circumstances which split up his seventeen-year marriage and separated him from his three children. 'It couldn't have been any different. What happened to me was the product of the person I was, the people we knew, the lives we'd led.'

No one else I spoke to felt quite so philosophical. But, while most did definitely feel regrets, often for their wives, always for their children, it certainly did seem, on following through their stories, that many fixed parts of their personalities learned from childhood could probably only have been altered or opened with outside help. (And no doubt that is also true of their wives, and the rest of us.)

While no one fault or failing, unless extreme in the extreme, is what breaks up a marriage, many strands did emerge from the stories I heard which, individually and collectively, seemed to contribute to the marriage breakdown.

## Failure to communicate feelings

So many men found it difficult to express their needs, desires, hurts and frustrations directly, very often because they weren't in touch with these themselves at the time and only started to become conscious of them after the experience of breakdown and divorce. They noted this themselves extremely strongly.

It is perhaps a truism now to say that males are brought up in a culture which demands that they be strong and protective and frowns on weaknesses but, although that is changing slightly, stereotypes die hard emotionally, if not intellectually, for both sexes. In the last decade, too, there has been much research by psychologists on sex differences in the development and organisation of the brain which, according to some well-renowned researchers, may explain why men and women have such traditionally different attitudes and interests. American researchers Diane McGuinness and Karl Pribram once summarised the sex-specific abilities of the brain to find that man is a 'manipulative animal' who expresses himself in action while woman is 'communicative', adept at receiving and transmitting. Men are more interested in objects than people, whereas women are the opposite, more responsive to emotional meaning. The conclusions – that these traits have a physical foundation – are still contentious and are admittedly a species-generalisation (all individuals vary) but they are intriguing and thought-provoking, especially in the light of so many men's own emotional experience.

It is only now, for instance, that Laurie, who stayed at home as the dutiful son till his mother died, recognises how little sense he had of his own inner world and how much he suppressed an anger and bitterness against his parents, particularly his mother, for denying him his own nature. When he did marry six months after her death, his emotions were firmly on hold. But he didn't know that then.

'It seemed to me that Carol and I had a very good relationship,' he said. 'We spent a lot of time together and we both liked doing things like going to the films and the theatre.

'But we were so naive. It appeared that everything was nice and normal because we didn't want to face any unpleasant things. I was all too aware, for instance, that we didn't have a good sexual relationship but I put it out of my head. I didn't want to look at it.

'We didn't talk about any problems, any differences. We never fought or argued. We just put the best face on everything. In my view, for instance, the idea of having children just never arose. I thought she didn't want them and she says, "What gave you that idea? You never asked me."

'I, of course, didn't think we had any problems and it was an incredible shock when finally I discovered that Carol wasn't happy at all. She had realised that her needs weren't being fulfilled, even though I still had no idea that mine weren't.

'I couldn't have told you, until years after we parted, why the marriage went wrong, or what had been in it for her. I contacted her to find out about the things we had never talked about, to throw light on why my second marriage seemed to be on the rocks. Carol said that, in marrying me, she felt she was running for shelter. She felt comfortable and safe with me, having had a turbulent and passionate relationship before which left her hurt. It had been safe for me too, unchallenging in some ways.

'We had almost an unspoken pact not to burst our bubble of cosiness and security. The big wedding, everything idyllic. We did have many things going for us but we were too alike temperamentally. We both needed to be brought out of ourselves.'

When psychologists carry out surveys as to why people are attracted to each other, high on the list of their findings is common interests – a link much more durable than first heady love or passion. But from Laurie's and others' experience, common interests cannot be the bedrock of a marriage if emotional honesty and openness are lacking. They can even serve to keep people emotionally apart. As another man recalled, 'When things were bad, we went out a lot and entertained a lot, because we couldn't bear to be left alone together.'

Like Laurie, Marcus, a tall, dark, quiet man now in his forties, says that he too had a deep inability to face or share his feelings, stemming from a homelife in which emotion was rarely expressed. He places that failure firmly at the root of his failed marriage. As a child, he had never performed sufficiently well academically to satisfy his scientist father. Pushed towards physics, yet naturally inclined towards literature, he had abandoned both to become a civil servant and only later had he followed his first love and taken up training as a teacher. When he met Rosalie, he was thirty-seven and a low-grade lecturer in American literature at a further education college. Rosalie was twenty-three, a former student of the college and then also a teacher. It was the attraction of opposites.

'She was very extrovert, very open about her feelings and I found that novel and refreshing, if somewhat frightening. I was very flattered that she was so taken by me,' he said. He was at the time still very insecure about himself and his abilities, although he hadn't acknowledged that in himself, and his failure to do so later led to marriage crisis. Instead, as he sees it now, he re-directed those feelings into a different feeling which was easier to handle, and enabled him to avoid the real source of conflict inside him. As he describes it:

'We had a ridiculously idyllic summer, marred only perhaps by my jealousy. I was extremely possessive and I was all too aware that other men paid her a lot of attention. But I feel now that all the jealousy was just a camouflage for real worries. It let me override the important things, like our age differences (Rosalie had lost her father when she was a child and I didn't want to face the fact that she might see me as a father figure), our entirely different backgrounds and the fact that I knew she wanted security and to settle down and have children, while I was nervous of responsibility altogether. I had been living with someone before and both of us had been more interested in our careers than children, we thought.

'I was playing. The jealousy was a way of feeling things, but not the right things. We had a terrific sexual rapport and in a way that got things out of perspective.'

He would have let things drift on in an aimless way but Rosalie was by then desperately keen to marry and have a baby. The baby, as it turned out, happened first and Marcus found that he was absolutely delighted. But then the pressures started. They had bought a flat which they sold, when two more children followed, to buy a small house. But unexpected survey problems meant they had had to drop the selling price of their flat and were left mortgaged to the hilt. They started to run up debts. Marcus did not earn a lot, Rosalie was no longer working, and so Marcus took a commission very gratefully, to write a popular book on his subject. But the book, which he had taken on to help money problems, just became an additional pressure because he found it very difficult to write. Problems became acute within his and Rosalie's marriage, and gradually led to its breakdown.

'One of the undoubted precipitating factors for me was the children – the sense of responsibility. And then my age bothered me. Because I had come to teaching late, I was on a low grade and not earning as I felt I should be, or providing for my family properly. (I considered that was *my* role. Rosalie hadn't wanted to work and although she would have been prepared to, I didn't want her to have to either.) I had never had much confidence in myself and I lost even more. I just found it impossible to write that book, and felt a terrible guilt because I knew I would miss the deadline.

'I became slowly terrified. I sat in my study at night and couldn't work. I did anything else but face the nightmare of that book. It seemed to represent me as I saw myself – a failure.

'Not surprisingly, Rosalie's insecurities were increasing, because of money and the children, and because her own insecure childhood left her needing more security than most, not less. I couldn't give it to her financially, I felt, and I wasn't giving it emotionally because I was so screwed up myself.

'She used to pour out her anxieties and talk and talk and talk. Then she'd feel relieved, while I ended up feeling slightly bruised and resentful. I didn't know why. I think I resented having to listen and listen, and then she felt fine and I no longer felt fine. Maybe I felt childishly ignored. I remember thinking of myself, "You shouldn't feel like that. It's ridiculous."

'I felt impotent because I was part of the problem. I resented the fact that she seemed to feel better and yet I hadn't done anything to change the situation.

'I became increasingly insecure about those emotional demands being made of me. Also, although I adored our children, I felt a bit resentful of them. I wanted attention and there was no time left for me, I felt. But I didn't ask for attention in the proper way at the proper time, either. I allowed myself to have all these reactions but I never said a word.'

Their sexual relationship had remained good till them. 'But now our problems started to come out there too,' said Marcus. 'It wasn't as spontaneous. I think I was looking for other things from lovemaking – security about my ability to provide and so on – and of course these don't come from sex. I remember feeling, after we made love, that I had been given something and that I hadn't given anything back. It was satisfying in a childlike way but worrying underneath.

'More and more Rosalie came to talk to me about things and I didn't give any response. She would say "Talk to me" and I didn't even know what she wanted me to say. I began to feel she was evil, that she was trying to conjure something from me that I couldn't give. It was very primitive but this is how I saw her – as trying to trap me.

'I was utterly incapable of talking about what was on my mind because then I'd have to look at it myself. And I was *so* shit-scared. So nothing was ever resolved and I talked less and less. I felt I was waiting for inspiration. I'd find the right thing to do and all would be well. But Rosalie's patience ran out.'

As for many men (and women) born into successful families, Marcus felt a very strong need to achieve and live up to others' expectations. At the time he didn't question his belief that he, as the male, should be the sole provider. His emotions were in conflict. He feared responsibility and yet believed he should shoulder it as a man. He felt he should be adult and do all the caring and was appalled to find that he also had the desire sometimes to be childish and cared for himself, in the way that his children were. But he couldn't identify and share those feelings which then exacerbated, and in turn were exacerbated by, Rosalie's own insecurities.

Some men felt that their lack of awareness of the importance of expressing feeling could be put down to their geographical or socio-economic backgrounds. But it seemed to me, hearing the same sorts of tales from such very different people, that the emotional climate at home was much more relevant than environment, education or income bracket.

Dan, whose father had died when he was a baby and whose mother effectively rejected him, married young mainly because he wanted a home. Like Laurie, he was attracted to his wife and liked her but, as he describes it, there seemed to be no strong deep feelings on either side. 'I was very fond of my son and fond of my wife but within a working class context,' he said. 'But you didn't think about that sort of thing. We just proceeded to get on with it. Neither of us worked at marriage. It was just "there".

'It fell apart eleven years later because a young girl fell in love with me. It was so marvellous to find someone found me so special and was so loving with me – a thing I had never had from anyone. As a child I had been derided all the time and my marriage had been functional, rather than affectionate.

'My wife was very like my mother – no touching, no kissing, no loving. I didn't know it was around to be had or that I could be the object of it.'

Frank, an editor in publishing, came from a very different background. His parents were well educated and reasonably well off and yet the emotional results, he felt, were the same. 'As children,' he said, 'we were never encouraged to express anger or tears. It was like living in an emotional straitjacket most of the time. It's a disaster, it all gets bottled up. So often we think it is all going to be different in our own marriages. But how can it be, when we haven't been trained to express ourselves?'

He married solicitor Sarah at twenty-eight, very much in love. 'But we didn't talk much about anything deep. We just thought it would all work out. Neither of us knew any divorced people and we had both come from stable homes.

'When things started getting difficult, we never discussed the fact that sexually we were becoming less and less active. It is so hard to be precise about what was happening but lack of communication was obviously the biggest problem. Neither of us talked to anyone else and we certainly didn't talk to each other. It might well have helped if one of us had had some close friend to talk to because then we might have found out where we were going wrong, which was not communicating. We just never realised we had wanted different things from the marriage.'

Frank and Steve, a man mentioned in the previous chapter who had married confidently at twenty-two, and thought divorces only happened in books, both used the word 'stable' to describe the homes in which they had been brought up. It is a word which conjures up the image of something very steady, very much on an even keel, impervious to the force of anything outside itself. Both grew up believing that that was the nature of marriage, rather than the nature of two particular individuals within a particular marriage.

Certainly Frank regarded the state of marriage as something with its own life which directed the individuals within it rather than vice versa. Like Dan, like many others, he didn't expect to have to work at and explore it.

Steve sees now that what he viewed as his being easy-going in his marriage might have appeared as lack of interest.

'I rarely get angry and I've never shown jealousy or felt it. I keep things I don't like about people to myself because I try to live and let live. People can't be what you want them to be but perhaps, then, they think you don't care.

'I never ever had rows with my wife. I hate rows. I prefer to walk away. Rows seem so futile. You end up saying things neither of you can cope with. One sees something as clear as daylight which the other won't ever see at all.'

Steve's way was to try to preserve a safe emotional distance but, as he himself reflects, it may have appeared that he didn't care enough to confront or confirm and put himself and his feelings on the line.

In retrospect, Stuart too feels that he took the state of marriage for granted in some respects. He was very much in love with his first wife, Celia, when he married her but he thought there was no need to express or reiterate that love in their life together. They had many shared interests and were good companions and he thought that was enough. Only now, very happily married for a second time, does he say of his first wife, 'We never discussed things. I only thought I was loving but I wasn't. I didn't share my feelings and I didn't say "I love you" enough. All the old clichés are true!

'For me, it is difficult to do, to show my affection. I felt embarrassed and that probably comes from when I was young. My parents didn't show lots of feelings. Concern, yes, but not feelings, so I was brought up with that. Also, I was an only child and that tends to make you more self-sufficient. You don't know how to show the kind of love and affection that brothers and sisters might express.

'I still find it hard to communicate physically. I don't hug easily. But I'm trying to correct that in this marriage and because we discuss it, because my wife *accepts* that I'm not as physical as she is, it isn't a problem as such. It doesn't mean I love my wife any the less. But in my first marriage, the matter was never mentioned and I'm sure it was a problem – but unspoken.'

Unlike Stuart, Frank, Dan and others, Ben was brought up in a home where there was more emotion than he could handle, but emotion of a hostile kind. His parents had argued and fought acrimoniously through his childhood and had ended by divorcing when Ben was still in his teens. His wife Gail had come from a very similar background and both felt very threatened by and fearful of uncontrolled anger. They swore they would never repeat the behaviour of their parents but, in so doing, suppressed the overt expression of any anger with each other that they felt. And in so doing, Ben feels now, their relationship became dishonest and their hostility covert. Ben said:

'When I didn't expose my anger – I didn't even know I felt angry – I just felt vengeful towards Gail. I'd just want to get back at her if she hurt me. Probably it would have been healthier to have been overtly angry and have big scenes – it would have stopped things dragging on with vague hopes that they would improve.

'Instead I stuck with the pledge we had both made not to get into rowing and violent accusations. We stuck with it, not for the sake of the children (we didn't have any), but for the sake of ourselves who were those children of a previous, similar set-up.

'We couldn't handle uncontrolled emotions because we equated those with hurt. That was the risky area.

'Now I've started to learn that you *can* get into really strong, highly irrational rows and the relationship can survive. Whereas for Gail and me, the avoidance of rows had to take the form of deceit.'

Perhaps strong feelings are only always threatening when expressed abusively and divisively, instead of constructively and through a wish to reduce distance rather than create it. Pete experienced the divisiveness of the dangerous kind first hand. He and Pam had resorted to mutual abuse.

'In that marriage, we were reduced to being absolutely awful to each other. You wouldn't think you could lose so much respect and say such things to hurt because you had been hurt yourself. We did still have some good times but there was no closeness. If you abuse each other like we did, you can't get close again,' he said.

Just as Marcus felt he had used jealousy to hide his real fears about his relationship, so Pete and Pam appeared to use abuse to hide hurt and thus also hid the source of the conflict.

More than anything else, poor communication was mentioned by men as a major contributory factor leading to marriage breakdown. Many were confronted by their wives or were begged to talk but felt unable to respond. They did not at that time have a vocabulary for their feelings, although the feelings, whether suppressed or denied, were still as strong. Most have felt a desire to change but not all.

Malcolm, the printer who was pessimistic about marriage from the outset, admits that he wasn't open about his feelings but doesn't feel any desire to change and is much happier divorced. 'I suppose it is bad for the relationship if you are not very open. But I don't think either of us made a very big effort. If you have to work at it so hard because it is so difficult, why bother? I don't have to work at being single! Why should I have to work at being married?'

## Not ready for marriage

One of the classic textbook problems for men is a feeling of being displaced when a partnership becomes a threesome. The advent of a child changes everyone's life but for men who do not play what they can see as an important role in baby and child care, one of their deeper feelings may be of loss rather than gain. They may feel responsible financially but not emotionally, and feel keenly the loss of their previous freedom.

It isn't only men, of course, who feel trapped. Women are nowadays just as likely to resent the loss of their career, mobility and freedom if they are at home bringing up a child. As Renate Olins, director of the London Marriage Guidance Council puts it: 'There has never been a formula for solution. It is just that people find it hard to accept that every decision to opt for one thing means giving up something else.'

Some men felt, in retrospect, that they had tried to combine the incompatible instead of settling for the consequences of choice, and that had put some pressures on their marriages.

Jeff was already a successful architect and having a good life as a single man when he married Kay at the age of twenty-seven. Although Kay was definitely the woman he wanted to be with, he felt that he had been pressured into marriage itself and then, within a year, pressured into a child, after which Kay gave up her job as an administrator. 'I then felt a bit left out and a bit uncared for. I considered I was generous to her and what I got back was little.' It wasn't until the baby was about eighteen months that Jeff started to feel like a father. Till then, he felt resentment.

'From being carefree, my life had changed. I now had a wife, a child and not all the love I wanted and so, all in all, it didn't feel very good.' Kay resented the fact that he didn't see any reason to change the kinds of activities he had enjoyed when single, such as spending the weekends flying. He had also enjoyed taking short-term work contracts abroad but, by the time their troubles came to a head, it was not just he and Kay who had to up sticks but he and Kay and three children. And whereas Kay had previously shared Jeff's spirit of adventure and enjoyment of change, she became increasingly uncomfortable at the up-rooting, and harboured resentment.

Coming too late to appreciate that he did want his wife and a family life was certainly, in Jeff's mind, one of several reasons why the marriage later foundered.

Dick, an electronics engineer, also became a reluctant father at twenty-eight. The relationship with his wife Ruth was rocky, and she had convinced him that what she needed to make her happy was a child. He had made it clear he didn't want to be responsible for bringing one up but Ruth said she would gladly handle all the practical side on her own. It didn't occur to either of them then that that was a risky compromise. And the baby, when born, drew them apart rather than together.

'When Tim was born, it was the most emotional experience of my life,' recalled Dick, 'but I didn't feel any special feelings for Tim when he was a baby. I felt he was Ruth's. I didn't want the role of father, which I saw as helping with all the shit, and we had agreed I wouldn't do that.

'I viewed it like this. In some families, babies are looked after by nannies who do all the physical things. I didn't feel my life would be enhanced as a human being by setting the washing machine to programme F and throwing in his dirty nappies.

'Ruth did want to talk about Tim a lot. If it was about things like his first sounds, I was interested. Most of the time it was about the mess he was making and I wasn't interested in that.

'He didn't interrupt my life. I just carried on with my electronics at nights, like I used to. I wasn't a very sociable sort of person and, when my relationship with Ruth had first started getting difficult, I had got into the habit of spending more and more of the evenings on my hobby. But there was considerable physical and emotional strain on Ruth, and that in turn put it on me.'

Both he and Ruth were well aware that having a baby had done nothing to solve underlying differences and it was, in fact, because of Dick's virtual absence as a father and lack of response to the child that Ruth eventually suggested they separate.

Many women, like Ruth, do press for a child in the belief that their husband's feelings will change once it is born. Dick's feelings did not change because, while with Ruth, he was shielded from responsibility and involvement. He only grew to know and love his son when he had to take some responsibility himself as an estranged parent.

Conversely, Tony who is Italian willingly embraced the responsibility of children but then came to regret it. He had married quite young and was enormously happy when his first child was born eighteen months later but when, three years on, Beth had their second, things subtly started to change for him.

'We were happy as parents,' he said. 'I loved the children and loved watching them growing up, but I wasn't really sharing their care. It was partly tradition and partly because I wasn't mature or ready enough, I think now.

'I was pulled away by all sorts of other activities with friends. I wanted to carry on as if I was single, and felt trapped. My wife must have resented it but she was very much a mother and put up with a lot without complaining. I think I withheld the expression of my feelings towards her in the last few years. Deep down I felt warm and attached but, at some point, I felt I hadn't experienced enough in the outside world, particularly with women, but also in terms of activities. There were 101 things you just couldn't drag a family along to.

'I started being attracted to other women. A lot of it was fantasy and I didn't have an affair. I took my wife for granted, I think, and she did complain at the end. But whenever she brought something up, I didn't want to know. I couldn't talk because I was so confused myself. I didn't know if I wanted to be a father, a family man and a lover, and I didn't want to ask myself the question either.

'I had met up with friends who were far more adventurous than I was and I was probably out of my depth. I tried drugs then for the first time, which added to my confusion. My wife didn't like that kind of hippie lifestyle, and there was terrible tension because of my attraction to other ladies. She felt insecure.

'Things got so bad that we both finally knew that something had to be done to save the relationship. We decided to change our lifestyle completely. I gave up my job in a large company and left my friends behind, and we moved to the country where I set up a craft shop. It was very exciting for a while, getting everything going, and I ceased to feel trapped.

'But, through the shop, I started meeting all sorts of interesting people, lots of women of course, and I might visit some after work for a coffee sometimes. I saw it as innocent but my wife resented it. In the back of my mind, I had a wanting. I enjoyed people's company but because my wife was family oriented, we had become insular. I wanted stimulation. Our relationship had never really been about talking and sharing ideas.

'Funny, in the last six months, I really thought things were getting better. I was happy with the direction our marriage was going and our social circle was widening through people at the shop. I was beginning to feel more relaxed about the way I was living, money problems had eased, and in that year I had sort of answered the questions I hadn't dared ask myself about what I wanted from life.

'I thought my wife was happier. It turned out she wasn't.'

Many men felt in retrospect that they hadn't experienced enough of freedom and life by the time that they got married, and not necessarily only those who had married young. Several felt resentful of the fact that they had been hurried on into having children, as they saw it, a resentment which added extra strain to the relationship even though they may have adored their children once born. Having children focused the fact that they had not resolved conflicts about responsibility and commitment.

Businessman Donald does not have children but he still wonders whether he will ever be 'ready' for marriage, as commitment is his struggle too. He feels that his difficult relationship with his mother when a child will permeate his attitude towards any relationship and he doesn't see how to change that. He was divorced from his wife after only two years.

His feelings about women as mothers are extremely strong. 'If you said "mothers are the root of all evil" to a woman, all hell would let loose,' he said cautiously, expecting an onslaught. 'They can't understand men's problems with mothers. They want to believe that they are doing a good job, when they bring up boys.

'I was an eldest son and my mother and I were always battling. We still do, even now. She had wanted me to conform and to fulfil her hopes and expectations and all my efforts not to were traumatic to her. When, as a student, I came home with a beard, my mother couldn't look at me without crying. She wasn't able to accept me as an individual.

'I see her as little as possible and even then we have to talk of neutral things, otherwise there is an emotional undertone. Not being able to cope with emotional blackmail is one of the reasons my marriage failed.

'I have a restless spirit which came from all our battles and I don't think that is necessarily a bad thing. I wonder if explorers had trouble with their mothers. But it made me unhappy with anything that smacked of loss of freedom.

'My mother didn't give me the freedom, the space, to love her. I think you need space to love, otherwise it slips into insecurity and demands for assurance of love. Because I couldn't commit myself wholeheartedly later, my wife needed the assurance of love and I couldn't really give it. I wasn't giving freely, I was giving from obligation.

'If you say this sort of thing to your parents, they'll say, "Of course we love you as you are." It is part of the process of emotional blackmail to keep you in that battle. For lots of people, it is never solved. It is one thing to know it, another to change it.

'Perhaps the only way to solve it is spiritually. Canoeing down the rapids, you are aware of your identity being closely related to your immediate environment and not all your past personal shit!'

## Mismatch of expectations

Do we marry people as they really are or as we would like to see them? It is not for nothing of course that expressions like 'love is blind' are so common in our parlance. Certainly many men I spoke to felt that they and their partners had not taken enough account of their very different ways of being or thinking or had failed, mutually, to accept, adapt and compromise. Some felt, looking back, rightly or wrongly, that their marriages were mismatches and nothing could have been done to change that – even though often the wives concerned didn't see things so blackly.

Bryan, a successful freelance graphic designer, feels that it was his wife rather than himself who was resistant to change. He admits, however, that he still feels very bitter about his divorce two years ago and finds it hard to be objective. 'I feel she was a hundred per cent to blame and that I'm totally innocent, whereas she feels the absolute reverse.' He married at thirty-five. 'I actually left it late to be sure of not making a mistake!' he hooted. 'I did make a mistake. I married potential. I married the person I hoped she would become.

'Cleo was very attractive, we shared a sense of humour and I saw her as someone who could do something with her life. She had a good job on a magazine but she gave that up as soon as she was pregnant – which was very soon, as we both wanted children – and never showed any interest in work again.

'She always seemed far more attached than was healthy to her parents and her brother and sister, who were both married with families. She put them before me, and ran to them for advice, whereas I had deliberately bust away from my own family to stand on my own two feet.

'She didn't seem to be interested in doing anything interesting or reading anything interesting. She wasn't that confident, whereas I was rather extrovert, and she didn't like going out anywhere, unless it involved her family. Most of the time, she won, but when she did give in and come to some do with me, she would flirt outrageously and that made me wild. I became very insecure.

'I felt she ceased to respect me or find me attractive. I know she says she felt I was far too critical of her and didn't let her be herself, that I always wanted to change her. But she was not a person to work at anything.

'It was a shock when she told me she didn't love me anymore because I did love her then. But now I feel hatred. I had felt there was just a switch to be thrown in her head somewhere, marked "aliveness". It happened sometimes and that was the person I wanted. That's what kept me wanting to stay together. Maybe it is only without me she will find her confidence and blossom.'

It is more usually women who wail to women's magazines, 'I thought I could change him' but the expectation is probably common to both sexes. One man said: 'Yes, I suppose I would have liked my wife to conform to the things I thought were reasonable. She could be very casual about things. She said that the more I tried to change her, the less she wanted to change. Changing was a big red flag to her and there wasn't any compromise or understanding on either of our parts.'

Angus, the systems analyst who had married sparkly, out-going Claire, had been aware that she was very moody and suffered 'the most phenomenal bouts of manic depression'. She had taken overdoses before he knew her and continued to do so periodically in their marriage. 'I would get home wondering what I would be greeted with. I had a terrible fear and yet, to her, it was almost normal. I had imagined that I was her knight in shining armour come to take her away from all that and, of course, it was fantasy stuff.' Instead, he found himself living with the reality of mental disorder which eventually took inevitable toll.

Dick, the electronics engineer who reluctantly agreed to a baby, was first strongly attracted towards Ruth, who was then a nurse, because she was so opposite from himself and the kinds of people he knew.

'She had an innocence, a basic simplicity and earthiness about her. She saw beauty and found joy in very simple things. I had just come back to England from travelling around Europe, where I had been into drugs and sex and knew a lot of strange people. My previous "relationships" had been with a mad Russian ballerina who couldn't speak English, and a French girl ten years older than me who seemed to have a penchant for nightclubs frequented by transsexuals. It was all mad, unreal stuff, all part of exploring life to the hilt.

'I had in no way been looking for someone like Ruth. But there was something unusually honest and, I thought, uncomplicated about her which I found very appealing. I found her very capable on a practical, organisational level, which I'm not, and I admired that. But later that side of her seemed to dominate her more and more and I found it increasingly difficult. I wanted the original spontaneity back, the part of her that I could respond to. Still, we were very happy for the first six months and decided to live together, even though something inside me, even when I was first attracted to her, said: "This isn't going to work." '

After a year it wasn't working. Dick only knew that he started to feel claustrophobic and the more attention Ruth wanted, the more he withdrew. Ruth increasingly felt that she must be at fault, that he was bored with her because she was not as intellectual as he was, and began to lose confidence in herself.

Dick admits he had become bored. Whereas, at the beginning, he was intensely involved and found 'a certain excitement in being the teacher, showing someone things I'd experienced and seeing them in a new light myself, I then wanted Ruth to be able to show *me* things in a new light. There was too much dependence on her side.' (He also recognises that he may have encouraged that by his initial keenness to lead.)

'We became more and more emotionally isolated and I spent more and more time apart from her at home, working on electronics projects. She wanted more attention and I wanted something that would *attract* my attention. Some comment that would make me think about anything of interest. There was no stimulation between us anymore.'

Yet he, as much as she, was reluctant to let the relationship go and felt there must be some formula to change it. 'It was when we started to talk about what was wrong that she said the biggest problem was she wanted a child and that that was what was making her demanding.

'I didn't want the responsibility, so why did I say okay? I thought she might be right. There was something very pure and warm and caring about her but also another part that was always searching for something. I didn't know what it was but I felt, if she found it, everything might come together.

'In retrospect, the alarm bells should have sounded. She did have a tremendous need in her life for something I couldn't fulfil but I didn't want to end the relationship. So it seemed the only thing to do.'

The first pregnancy ended in miscarriage and it was after that that Dick asked Ruth to marry him. 'She had said, after the miscarriage, that she felt insecure because we weren't married. So I decided, when we were trying again for a child, the best thing we could do was get married. With all the difficulties of having a child, the last thing she needed was the insecurity of worrying whether I'd still be around.

'By then I was on a treadmill where I felt that if I could just eliminate all these kinds of obstacles – the insecurity, the not having a baby, etc – that had got in the way of a very good relationship, it could all go back to how it was. I wouldn't let it sink in that we were unsuited.

'After the baby was born and nothing was any better, Ruth said she felt we needed more space and that she would be able to relax and start to enjoy life again if we moved to a bigger place. It was then I started to doubt that there was any exterior means of solving our problems and we could spend our whole lives finding supposed solutions which made things worse. I liked our place. But she felt a move was needed, so move we did. I resented it.

'The relationship had become so irrational that moving was just a symbol of our inability to solve anything. I think we both knew the relationship couldn't work.'

At the time it was by no means blindingly clear to either Dick or Ruth that they were looking for excuses or rationales outside of themselves to explain why their relationship was no longer fulfilling. As marriage guidance counsellors commonly find, it is often easier or more comfortable for couples to deflect attention from the real source of conflict – themselves – than fully confront it; and, while caught up in the collusion, impossible to see.

As might be expected, many couples found that their interests simply diverged, or were always divergent but time had taken away the high passion or excitement and novelty that had disguised that, and the interest that might have enabled them to probe deeper.

Charles, who had married with great trepidation at thirty-seven, felt that, very quickly after their children were toddlers, he and Deborah ceased to have much to say to each other.

'We were metabolically so different, to boot,' he said. 'I've got nervous energy, leap up early and run out of steam in the evenings. Deborah was the reverse. It would agitate me that she was a zombie till noon and then, in the evening, it was party time for her but not me. This caused irritation until I realised I was just dealing with a different type of person. I had thought all normal people were like me! But discovering she had a different metabolism had a distancing effect. I felt I couldn't do anything about it and therefore I couldn't have an energetic companion.

'The chemistry wasn't there either. She is not my type sexually and probably vice versa. But I only know this now because I have met my "type" since. At the time I didn't even know enough to talk about it.

'We couldn't agree on friends to invite to dinner because the kinds of people we wanted to be with were different. Mine were business people, hers were more teacher types. She had got a job as a nursery school teacher herself. That was another thing. I was glad she had got a career for herself and encouraged it, but it did mean our lives would go more apart. I felt her interest in the house reduced and I wasn't getting the back-up I needed in my career. Little things, like there being no one to take my stuff to the dry cleaners.

'Very slowly our lives separated and then I started affairs. I didn't know what I was looking for. The last thing I wanted was to break up my marriage. But I was being driven by some inner need, partly for sex and partly for companionship.'

He remains convinced that their lack of communication was a chasm that could not have been bridged. 'Lack of communication? To say that implies you can have it. I think that, between the two people we were, communication wasn't possible.'

Dave, a biochemist working in industry, has similar feelings. He is now forty-one, married twenty years ago and has been divorced from his wife for a few years. 'Anthea really became depressed during her fourth pregnancy. We hadn't planned it and she had wanted to return to part-time work as an arts administrator. We didn't take holidays because it was so difficult with so many youngsters – we had only been married six years. She felt she never got away from things.

'My wife didn't have any hobbies. I said, "You must do something. Don't let yourself be housebound." At my coaxing, she took up a pottery class one evening a week, which she really enjoyed, but when it closed because of lack of people, she didn't seem bothered and didn't try to find something else.

'I enjoyed working on my home computer. I found it a great way to relax. But that meant that, even though I was at home, I wasn't communicating with her and she did resent it a bit. But within a year of our last child, our interests were so different that communication had suffered anyway. I started losing interest in her. We didn't speak the same language. Her upbringing had been different. She loved opera and ballet, which were alien to me, but had no interest in scientific things, which I was fascinated by.

'We started having rows over the fact that she was left with the children while I could escape to work. That must happen so often and is so unfair on the woman. She did start work when the youngest started nursery school and that helped us a bit. But she did nothing in the house at all, whether she was working or not. She didn't mind living in a mess – her parents' house had been like that – but I hated it. I used to come home from work and do all the clearing and washing up that was piled there. I didn't mind that, I like things clean although I don't mind them untidy, but it was just that we had such different ways of liking to live.

'Nothing happened suddenly. We just gradually communicated less and less and I ceased to have any interest in her at all. She did have a genuine affection towards me but I couldn't return it. We were rapidly getting to the stage where I'd had enough. One day it hit me when I left work that I didn't actually *want* to go home.

'There was not a lot left in the marriage for me besides the children, although we did stay together for seventeen years. I had seen a lot of marriages going downhill, so it wasn't that I expected a lot. This was just, as I thought, what marriage was like.'

I was struck by the fact that neither Charles nor Dave tried to give justifications for their very strong negative feelings about their wives as partners in order to show themselves in a better light. Both were, in their own minds, the 'guilty' parties as far as precipitating the final marriage breakdown was concerned. And both, in fact, have very reasonable relationships now with their ex-wives. They felt, more strongly than anyone else I spoke to, that a true basis for happiness in their marriages was lacking and, having poor expectations, did not feel they could have significantly improved them. And that is not to say that they didn't find their marriage breakdown deeply painful at the time.

Sometimes couples appeared to have made assumptions about each other's lifestyles, wants and aims on very limited evidence. Frank, the publisher who had come from a stable home, puts that down to his and his wife's expectation that marriage just 'worked'. They chose to ignore or downplay potential areas of conflict, seeming to each other more like-minded than they actually were.

'There was no one point at which it suddenly went wrong,' he said of his thirteen-year marriage to solicitor Sarah. 'I sometimes think there was a slow deterioration from the moment we married. I took her for granted. I can be very bad tempered and criticise easily, which I wasn't aware of at the time, and she reacted to criticism badly.

'We had had this idealised picture of what marriage would be like and this wasn't it. We had known each other a few years beforehand but, because we lived quite far from each other, we didn't see each other that often and, when we did, we met somewhere in the middle and then came back to my house. I like going out and I thought that when we married, we would be able to go out more. She thought, when we married, we wouldn't have to go out so much. This was the kind of misunderstanding we had, things we never talked about.

'We disagreed over lots of things. She liked things organised, I liked things spontaneous. It was a major difference between us which affected many things – holidays, what friends we had, everything.'

The shock discovery that he had married a different person from the one he had expected was also what set Donald's marriage to Joanna, a radiotherapist, on the downhill track. He, with his restless spirit that he believes was fostered by his battles with his mother for independence, had a horror of suburban family life and the patterns of routine. 'Joanna was in love with the idea of being married and had romantic notions of suburban existence which I just didn't take seriously. When we were going out, I was the centre of her world because I was her passport to what she wanted. So what I said went. She was willing to do and go where I wanted and appeared to enjoy it. That disguised the fact that we had very different characters.

'Once we married, she had achieved her objective and gradually asserted her real self. She wanted to have the same friends to dinner parties, do the same things, go to the same places on holiday. I found it more exciting to meet new people and go to new places. I was an embarrassment because I wanted to explore the limits of things while she wanted to be conservative, domestic and have children.

'We were living in a flat. She wanted to move to a house but I wouldn't. The flat was convenient and I didn't want to move till I found something which I felt would answer our needs – a whole house that wasn't in suburbia, where there was enough space to be apart and have children. But a place like that would have cost three times as much in London and I didn't want to be mortgaged up to the hilt. She would go to other people's houses and say how wonderful they were and I felt it was emotional blackmail.

'The question of children came up early on. She did want them but I thought we had plenty of time and we couldn't have had them in the flat. I didn't desperately want children myself. I found the responsibility a commitment difficult to make. But we never discussed it all that seriously.

'I travelled quite a lot in my job as an oil company executive and we wouldn't have survived the two years if I hadn't. To me, it was pretty obvious it was a fiasco early on. Even our strong sexual attraction hadn't lasted. I don't know if she had only been enthusiastic before because it was part of the getting married deal. Later she saw it as an exercise in reassurances, not enjoyment, so that was emotional blackmail again, as far as I was concerned.'

He is perfectly well aware that he was unwilling to, or incapable of, compromise and that he caused Joanna considerable pain, more than he had to experience himself. He explains rather than excuses himself, because he doesn't feel he could have acted differently.

'For me, if the marriage wasn't working, it didn't overly matter. I had work, travel, the occasional fling. Men have found a way of living in marriage and getting things outside it. It's a support system, not a commitment system, to them. Whereas for women it is a very important part of their life and the more economic freedom they have, the less they will tolerate men not fulfilling what they want.

'Joanna's life was marriage, whereas I hadn't put emotional commitment into it. Adjusting to the idea of not being married, when we were splitting up, was terribly difficult for her.'

The boot was on the other foot for Robert, who had joined the army to escape his awful homelife and hankered after a real home when he left it. 'I settled down very quickly when I got married at twenty. I thought we were happy. We spent our time working on the flat, watching TV. It was all mundane stuff but not boring to me. I felt I had lived before marriage and this was settling down. I was really happy just to be at home. I didn't even go out drinking like I used to. But my wife must have felt bored, I suppose. She wanted to go out and have fun.'

## Ignoring one's own needs

Many women feel that, as wives and mothers, they tend to put their own emotional needs second. They may find themselves supporting men in all other ways than financial, and often sharing that side too. But men suppress needs as well, different needs which often they don't even realise they have a right to, again because of cultural demands on men to have the strong shoulder, take it on the chin and not show unmanly feelings like hurt and fear.

Pete, who thought success was having his own house at twenty-one, didn't recognise his own need to feel wanted. He thought that his hurt and resentment about his wife Pam's extremely flirtatious behaviour meant that he was weak and unmanly.

'Pam's mother had always been the boss in their house and Pam used to want to dominate me. We had lots of rows which always ended with her threatening to leave me and as I didn't want that, it was always me who backed down. I felt a lesser person than her. She could always make me feel small. I felt at that time that in relationships one person cares and one doesn't care, and the carer has to keep it together, but that if it came to the crunch the carer would lose. I wasn't that comfortable as a person then. I always felt I must be wrong because I didn't know what else there was. I didn't know there was a life where you don't have confrontations, I thought it was all winners and losers.

'Pam and I would go to parties on the estate where we lived. I hated them. She looked really sexy and I didn't appreciate the attention she got and how she liked it. It's belittling. It makes you feel so bad inside, watching your wife necking with other people's husbands.

'You were thought a pillock if you danced with your own wife. The ethos was, just enjoy it, it doesn't *mean* anything if people grope your missus and she enjoys it. But it does. I used to go mad when we got home. I'd say, "Why do you do it?" "What?" she'd say. "Nothing wrong with that. It's a party for godsake. What's wrong with *you*?"

'The couples who didn't do that sort of thing didn't go to those parties, I suppose. But I didn't know that. I thought everyone did it. I felt it was me who was in the wrong again.'

He always felt little in comparison with his wife, even though he is well-built, over six foot, very good-looking and, to outsiders, definitely his own man. Sexually he developed a poor image of himself.

A couple of other men specifically mentioned feeling far more sexually insecure than outward appearance and attitude might have indicated. They and their wives saw themselves as modern and open-minded, keen to remove traditional restraints from marriage and allow each other to develop as individuals. That included allowing sexual encounters with other partners. Jealousy rather than infidelity was taboo. But, as the men found, lust without love was not such an easy option for them, and because that failure didn't accord with their image of the times, their masculinity felt threatened.

Ben started to seek sex with other women after his wife Gail started seeing other men. For all his then debonair demeanour, he was 'seeking some kind of comfort and reassurance as a male. But we were both filled with the '70's propaganda of the open marriage. We were just drifting along with the atmosphere of the times – explore, don't be scared to. But it was all far more difficult for me than for Gail, because I had had a puritan background.

'We said, effectively, "I don't mind if you have an affair with someone else but don't tell me the details." I certainly don't feel that way now. I think, in my flings, I was looking to find out more about women and about myself because I was being challenged by Gail on a sexual level. I was less attractive to her than someone outside. But a lot of it was just vengeful against Gail – "I'll show you!"

'I don't think I consciously felt jealous when it was open. But I did mind when she lied to me, like when she said she would be back at 10 p.m. and then got back at 3 a.m., saying the car had broken down. I can recall fury but no confrontation, because we were both nervous of anger, and because I was on automatic pilot. I remember thinking of myself as a robot husband, being used as her machine to keep the household going but the good times weren't for me.

'I tried to ignore the fact I cared. It was all supposed to be so adult.'

Scriptwriter Morris, immensely articulate and droll and very self-deprecating about his behaviour in marriage, has similar feelings about conning himself into living up to the macho expectations, although he feels he was more to blame than his wife. 'We both had one-night stands. It was the thing to do to prove how bohemian we were. The hippies were arriving and we were very tuned to all that, and greeted it with public shouts of joy, but fewer private ones.

'I was continuously frightened that I wouldn't prove satisfactory to my sexual partners. Even one-night stands left me with incredible post-coital depression. It took me an awful long time to realise this was a signal that really I was only comfortable as a monogamous person.

'I didn't trust my wife because she had flings. I ignored the fact that I was having them too – a complete double standard.'

A number of men felt obliged to be caring and strong, to the exclusion of their own needs. Angus feels this was very much the case in his marriage to Claire, the exuberant dark-haired beauty who also had overwhelming fits of despair and several times tried to commit suicide.

'All feelings were Claire-oriented, mine were left out – although I didn't know what my feelings were,' he said. 'It had been part of my upbringing not to consider my feelings.

'It seemed hers was a demanding existence I had to support. She took overdoses to escape, sleep, not to die. The ambulances late at night, the neighbours watching, it was all hideously embarrassing. Then, at work, I'd get called to her from meetings, it was very hard to cope with.

'Neither of us really understand what she felt so despondent about. She was having therapy, and had electro-convulsive therapy loads of times, but it seemed as if the issues were being skirted. At times she was effectively an invalid, other times she was really happy. She never accused me of anything or was in any way hateful towards me.

'Within two or three years I knew I couldn't cope. I wanted a way out of the problems but not the marriage. I remember one time when she got so hysterical in a shop and started behaving so oddly (I wasn't there) that the police were called. She went so berserk with fear that she ended up in a cell.

'For my part, it can't have been all agony or I wouldn't have been there. But after a while I began to become aware of my own needs and feelings. I was a person too and had my own rights to happiness. I realised I wasn't a saint and didn't want to be one. Once that revelation came, it seemed pointless to continue. We had no children. We split up after seven or eight years.'

Stuart's wife also had intensive psychiatric treatment a few years after they married. 'She had had a very difficult childhood and her father had had psychiatric problems,' he said. 'She became very dependent on me and it felt okay at the time to me that she was dependent. At the time you just go along with it. I found myself looking for what I thought *she* needed or wanted and that actually caused strain and confusion. I felt I needed to be more caring towards her, whereas she felt smothered because she really wanted to be more independent. And that made me feel rejected.

'I wish I'd done more things. I never really travelled and I've never lived anywhere but the North. I turned down a job in the South because of Celia's illness. But I never even voiced my wish to go, so it wasn't my wife's fault, it was mine. I put the limitations on my own life because of how I saw our life at that time.'

In a somewhat similar way, Dick avoided looking at what he wanted out of marriage by seeing the 'problems' as all his wife Ruth's. If *she* could be made to feel secure, by marriage, by having a baby, by moving to a bigger place, that would be the solution. But she resented feeling that her insecurities were all to blame, felt even more inadequate, and so no dialogue about mutual needs ever really ensued. But, as Dick saw it at the time, 'I tried to support her, do the best for her.'

Jay, the deputy headmaster, encapsulates the consequences of that very clearly. 'I realised eventually that in my marriages and other major relationships, I couldn't admit how *I* felt things ought to be. I would try to please, be nice, care more about the other. But that's a disaster for the other person too, because then they can't define themselves. It is like spoiling a child. There's nothing for them to come up against.

'The unwritten contract in both my marriages was that I was strong and didn't need supporting. Shelley, my second wife, wanted fathering and I remember a friend of mine saying, when he met her, "Oh God, you've done it again." They couldn't take the real me and I didn't know who the real me was either, except that early on I realised that, if I displayed any weakness, that wasn't acceptable. But I had no clear idea of what I had a right to expect out of a relationship.'

He was very much in love with Shelley, a PR executive, very powerfully attracted to her and very keen for her to have his children. But the first pregnancy ended in stillbirth which was devastating to them both.

'It was terrible having to phone her parents and mine, and then to meet people in the street the day after, who smiled in anticipation of being told it was a boy or a girl. I couldn't bear the thought of going into school without my colleagues knowing, so I had phoned my boss to let him know, and let others know, in advance. They were very upset for me and decided it was best not to mention the matter, so I got no compassion at all. I was the one who had to broach it and reassure *them*. I was also busy caring for Shelley and her feelings and spent so much time reassuring others that I didn't grieve properly myself.

'We did have another child but it was only when our marriage had gone wrong shortly after, and I was clinically depressed, that I ended up seeing a doctor, and all my feelings about our stillborn came out. Everything was released and I cried and cried and cried for the first time. I sort of went on crying for six years and I'm still emotional about it now. Whereas Shelley had been able to work through her grief at the time.

'I feel I know the needs I have much better now. I know I need some mothering too, I've been looking after others too long. I've also learned to say no to things I don't like and it's rather nice. I do wonder why it has taken me so long to get a clear image of myself. Perhaps it was because I was brought up in cotton wool. My parents never rowed in front of us and I didn't know it was okay to have a screaming argument. I grew up without an understanding of the range of human emotions. I didn't know how to handle them – and probably still don't, in some ways.'

Jay's story illustrates very powerfully the force of the still pervasive image that strong men don't cry. Because he saw his role as comforter and supporter, responding to Shelley's more accessible and external show of pain, he allowed himself no chance to get fully in touch with his own feelings. He thought he had acknowledged and handled his sadness without the need to express it in a typically 'female' way. Yet, without a full outlet, the emotions escalated inside him and the unidentified pain permeated every corner of his life.

For many people, the strong emotional shock of loss of someone close to one or both partners appeared to precipitate a breakdown in their relationship. The tension, strain, disorientation and misery may pervade every pocket of life and so it seems that the marriage itself is a source of conflict instead of a source of comfort. Extreme sorrows such as stillbirths, repeated miscarriages, failure to get pregnant and the death of a husband or wife's mother or father all took immediate toll in some marriages.

Bill, a painter and decorator, said: 'Louise's mother died suddenly and she became very depressed. Her attitude just changed. Even her sister said she was a different person.' Bill has no conception that anything was actually wrong with their marriage before. 'I loved her. We had been married twelve years. I still bought her flowers every couple of weeks and, whenever I bought sweets for the children, I always bought chocolates for her. We went out together regularly.

'The Christmas before her mum died, she sent me a card saying she was more in love with me then than ever before in our marriage. Now it's all gone, wallop. She didn't know what was the matter but, if I tried to talk, she didn't want to know. Three months later I caught her with another man.'

Joe felt his wife changed towards him almost inexplicably after a third pregnancy that ended in stillbirth. 'The stillbirth really cut us both up. I was told to expect that she would go through a really bad depression. She did and I accepted that. But it just went on and on. She behaved as if I wasn't there and after a year I suggested I left for a couple of months, just to give us a break so that we could make a clean start. But the break became permanent.'

Others felt aware, however, that the emotional crisis, usually of death, served to take off the lid of a cauldron of discontent that was already bubbling below, for one or both partners.

## What about the wife's needs?

'Of course, she probably didn't see it like that', many men said as they described their own sides of their stories. But most were aware that, whatever lack of fulfilment they had experienced, their wives had felt equally bereft in various ways, although it was a shock to some to be told at the end that their wives felt unloved, excluded or taken for granted. Some simply couldn't understand why.

Men who put emphasis on their work or careers, for instance, tended to feel hurt that their wives said they had felt lonely or left out. Charles said: 'Deborah did complain later that I was married to my career and not to her. But I don't think women like her realise what career imperatives a man can be under. So I felt a lack of appreciation from her. I felt I was doing a lot for my family, as well as satisfying my own ambitions. Yes, I got job satisfaction, but I didn't spend money on me. It all went on the home and family.' In his eyes that was a fair, even noble, exchange.

Other men, too, said that they worked all hours to afford to build up a nice home and give things to their families. Looking back, Pete says: 'I was permanently working virtually seven days a week until two years before we split up. The excuse was I was working for us. In reality it was probably ambition.' Another man said: 'My wife used to go on holidays alone. I never go on holidays. I'm the breadwinner and the more I can earn, the more I can build the home up.' Reading between the lines, it is probably fair to say that a number of wives, especially those at home with children, came to feel they wanted more from marriage than money, even if they enjoyed the things that money could buy.

It was only in retrospect that most men could say that they *had* taken their wives for granted, expected too much, been too selfish or not loving enough. None really felt blameless, with the benefit of hindsight, and some felt, probably far too much, that they themselves were almost or entirely to blame.

# ══ 3 ══
# The affair

'Celia was often in tears but till then we had never really discussed what was wrong. She said she didn't find our lovemaking pleasurable any more and then we did talk and decided on some time apart. I didn't even know then she was having an affair. All I know is that she rang me two weeks later and wanted to end our marriage.

'It was a while after we split up that my sister-in-law told me about the affair. Celia had got involved with a friend of mine, who was married with children, but he wouldn't leave his wife for her. I felt shock that it was my friend, not shock that she had been having an affair.

'Her having an affair was just a symptom of the breakdown of our marriage, as far as I was concerned.'

Stuart, a quiet undemonstrative man, was speaking calmly, with six years between him and the break up of his marriage, the last four spent in very happy marriage to someone else. But while affairs within other marriages brought much stronger reactions and sometimes led directly to the break, they were almost always seen as a symptom of breakdown, as Stuart put it, rather than the cause. Only one or two men had had no idea anything was wrong before their wives started affairs.

Very rarely, however, could husband or wife cope with the emotional consequences of their partner's affair which usually served to put the spotlight on all that had been wrong or lacking before but shelved by one or both. 'We stood there glaring at each other,' said one man, 'Then suddenly she burst into tears and wailed "but I love him!" It was a terrible shock. I realised I had been duped. But far worse was the realisation that she would never have cried over me like that. I had so much wanted her to feel like that about me.'

Another: 'She had been depressed and withdrawn for some time but I couldn't get her to tell me why. Then I caught her kissing another bloke. I was really angry with her. But what hurt the most was that she was showing a hell of a lot of feeling while kissing that man.'

As might be expected, in a book about divorced men, even those who decided to try again afterwards did not manage to alter the pattern of their relationships significantly enough to save their marriages. Whatever the outcome, men varied markedly in their immediate responses to wives' affairs and had a number of different attitudes to embarking on their own.

## The other man

The sudden discovery of an affair was inevitably a shock, particularly if a wife was caught red-handed, but very few men, far fewer than I had expected, expressed their feelings physically. Most remembered feeling numbed. It was perhaps more instinctive or safer to go into emotional freeze than to unleash what would have been extremely charged, powerful and perhaps dangerous emotions.

Maybe men are more frightened of what they are capable of physically but, as Renate Olins, Director of the London Marriage Guidance Council, pointed out: 'I think we *all* have difficulty dealing with very powerful anger. What can you do that can adequately express it, without picking up a meat cleaver. Because it is all so overwhelming, we often do nothing.'

Ben felt overwhelmed. He and Gail, pushed along by the '70's propaganda of open marriage, as he put it, had both continued to have affairs within their own. But Ben had become less and less capable of pretending to himself that this was adult behaviour, and felt more and more inadequate over Gail's seemingly intense need to look for sexual satisfaction elsewhere. Then he himself met a woman with whom, for the first time in his own foray into flings, he became emotionally involved, but the guilt and uncertainty on both sides brought it to a stop.

'Gail knew about her and had started to feel threatened. She had been having some pretty unhappy affairs herself. We went away on a holiday together, had a real talk and decided that, from now on we would be together properly, no more explorations,' he said. 'It felt like a good decision. I felt we both meant it.'

Then Ben had to be away on business. 'When I came back, I found someone else's sock in the bedroom. I was really out of my head with upset but I didn't say anything at all. I was so hurt and didn't know what to do because we had just made this big promise. A couple of really good friends said, "Why bother with it?" "You're an idiot." In the end I just left without fully confronting her. I just told her I didn't want to live with her anymore, I couldn't believe her anymore.

'She admitted there had been a man there but she was terribly upset at my going. I didn't ask who the man was, I had never cared to know. A lot of time had been wasted on our avoiding confrontation. But that was to do with our personalities. We would do anything rather than have a real row.'

Joe's wife had become extremely depressed when her third pregnancy had ended in stillbirth and when, after a year, nothing had improved ('She behaved as if I wasn't there'), he offered to move out for a while.

'I came and saw the children every other Sunday. It was awful. They cried at the door each time I left them and I cried when I got out of sight down the road. It was a really bad time but she wouldn't go to the doctor or anything.

'After a couple of months I had to go to the house unannounced to collect something and found my best mate in my bed. He was also my assistant at work. I was numb. I couldn't do or say anything. A few pieces fell into place. I just left straightaway and went and had a very long talk with the bloke whose house I'd been staying in.

'I never saw my mate again because I jacked in my job. I wish I had been angry. I felt later I should have socked him just for self satisfaction,' said Joe, a well-built man who looks as though he could pack a powerful punch if he wanted to. 'I saw a bloke who looked like him recently (fifteen years later). I thought again, I wish I'd socked him.'

Robert, the sad-eyed builder who had so wanted his own home, is not a big man but he is afraid of his anger. Yet he also felt numb when he found his wife in bed with another man.

As far as he was concerned, 'everything seemed rosy' when he and his wife were living in the house they had finally won from the council with their very young daughter. He was only too happy for his life to revolve around the home and they had no money to go out anyway. He was twenty-one and his wife nineteen, and she felt considerably more restless. She wanted to start working part-time behind a bar, ostensibly because money was tight, although Robert has his doubts about that now. Then she also started going out on other nights with her sister, who was recently divorced and had two children. Robert babysat.

'I didn't feel used. I felt left out. We started arguing. Our sex life had got dull, she wasn't interested any more whereas before it was great. I was put in second or third place all the time and I didn't seem to enter her life at all. Only if she had any room over might she find time for me.

'She was working quite a few nights a week by then. I remember talking to her sister, trying to find out where we were going wrong, and she said I shouldn't be so dominating, I should let my wife have some freedom. So I agreed to the nights out, while I stayed home with the baby. But she started coming home later and later and we hardly saw each other. Because I was so frustrated I started going out drinking on the few nights she was in.

'I was like a lamb being led to slaughter. I never thought she would be interested in other men, although I was starting to feel suspicious.'

He was finally persuaded by his wife, he says, to go away for a while and 'give the marriage a chance to work after the dust had settled. But I missed my daughter so much, I felt I had to go back.'

He had been staying with his sister in London but when he finally decided he could stand it no more, he caught the first train back. 'It was a milk train really. It arrived very early in the morning.' He doesn't know if, subconsciously, he deliberately got that train.

When he got back, he found the front and back doors bolted. 'That annoyed me. I couldn't even get in my own front door. There was only a top bedroom window open and for me it was easy to shin up the drainpipe, being in building.

'It was the back bedroom, where our daughter slept and my wife's sister's kids were there, because she was staying too, but they didn't wake up. I went to my bedroom and there she was, my wife with another man.

'I felt disgust, shock, horror – and also a relief, because all my suspicions had been confirmed and it was all over. They woke up but I just left them and went downstairs. No, I didn't yell. I suppose I didn't want to wake the children.

'I made myself a cup of tea. Eventually my wife came down. She was only apologetic to the extent that I'd actually caught her. That was it for me. I made arrangements to go back to London to get over the shock.'

Robert very much wanted his daughter and did, in fact, win custody of the child. But he knew he still loved his wife, regardless of what she had done to him, and wanted a reconciliation, so, when she came back and said she was sorry 'it was a dream come true. She had seen the error of her ways and I was prepared to forgive and forget.

'We agreed we would go out together and not separately in future and we made a go of things. I felt I had to give her more leeway and not be possessive. For instance, she felt she had to continue working at the bar but said it was purely for financial reasons this time, and occasionally she would babysit for her sister.

'Then she started coming home later and later from the babysitting and my suspicions started getting aroused and we started arguing again. It had happened before, so it was like pieces in a jigsaw, but she denied it all of course.

'And then I started doubting myself. She made me feel guilty for suspecting her. How could I be such a bastard, she'd say, and not trust her when we were starting over again?

'It went on for a few months. One night I was alone. She had taken Mandy, our daughter, with her to her sister's, as company for Mandy's cousins, she said. Mandy was going to sleep over if it got late but the sister's boyfriend would run my wife home.

'Pub closing time came and went. But then I thought, perhaps the sister and her boyfriend had gone for a meal afterwards. However, at 2 a.m. I had had enough. I walked to the sister's house, ten minutes away, and hammered till I got an answer. My wife came down in a dressing gown and we argued on the doorstep. I accused her of having another affair and she denied it.

'I got past her and looked around downstairs. She wouldn't let me upstairs, saying she didn't want the children woken up. She begged me not to go up, but I went. In the spare bedroom, I found nothing. I went downstairs and apologised to her for being so suspicious. I should have realised she had just decided to stay the night (we didn't have a phone) and instead I had come barging in like a bull. I was sorry.

'She was trying to calm me down, because I had been so angry and I was in a state. And then I saw a pair of shoes which weren't the sister's boyfriend's because he was big. All my suspicions were aroused again and I went back upstairs and found the man under the bed.

'I wasn't angry then. I think all the anger had gone out of me when I had been trying to confirm my suspicions. Once confirmed, there seemed no point in expressing anger.

'I think I just went back home. I felt suicidal. Suspicion is like having a missing piece in a jigsaw and you can't complete the picture until you have got that final piece. I know things hadn't been brilliant between us but I hadn't expected they would be. We had been having little sex – she was either tired or like a sack of potatoes, which didn't do my ego much good and I'd even started suffering from premature ejaculation. But I had thought things would improve in time. I now realised she was quite happy to go on having affairs and had made no real effort at all to save our marriage.'

Robert has since recognised the dangers for him of suppressing his feelings. (He developed severe ulcers.) 'I thought I had a very long temper and could take and take and take but that isn't always the case. I think I've got it under control, because I'm afraid of what I could do in anger. I believe no man should hit any woman regardless of the situation. That tends to devalue your own feelings for yourself. But I do feel I have been extremely provoked and on many occasions now I'll punch a door just to get the physical aggression out of me, rather than having it sit on my chest as tension.'

Pete, who had felt so belittled by his wife Pam's behaviour at parties, did experience anger with her over that but when she finally told him of an important affair with another man, he ceased to be in touch with his pain at all. 'I went round to see the man, who was my neighbour. I told him I thought he was scum. I wanted to fight him then because he was angry and excited, but I was ice-cold and knew I could take him. Then Pam intervened, all upset and I just said, "Oh, isn't that dramatic!" and walked out.'

Steve was most aware of a terrible sense of powerlessness when his wife told him, out of the blue as far as he was concerned, that she was having an affair with another man. She had come home at 6 a.m.

'It was an enormous shock. She had always accused me of being the one who might have an affair because I met famous people (he works in the film industry) but I was never interested. As I've said before, when I met her, at twenty-two, I felt I wanted to be with her exclusively for the rest of my life.

'I knew the man concerned and I knew that, for him, it would be just another in a whole string of affairs but when I told her that, she wouldn't have it. She refused to stop seeing him and went to stay at her sister's and that was the end of the marriage. She wanted to come back six weeks later but it was too late. It had destroyed my trust. It blew me to pieces. The difficulty was my powerlessness in it all. You think you can cope with anything but this was out of my hands.

'I couldn't stop feeling the way I had about her but I had an awful lot of pride. For me, once the unwritten rules are broken, that's it. Otherwise it will happen again. In a month's time there could be another one.

'I rarely get angry but if I do, once in a couple of years, I could kill. I wanted to kill my wife's bloke, not her. (I never felt any anger towards her.) But very quickly, I just found him laughable really.'

Only two men recalled really fully giving vent to their feelings, at any point. Pete remembers very clearly the last New Year's Eve party he went to with Pam where he saw her not flirting with everyone but 'necking and snogging with just this one guy'. He didn't know then that they were having an affair.

'I looked around and saw her and I couldn't stand it. I still thought I wasn't supposed to care and all that, it was just a party, but I bloody well did. I went over and told her, hadn't she better check the kids. She said yes and set out to go across the road to our house but I followed her out and told her she wasn't going back.

'Her eyes glittered with rage. "You're joking!" she said, "fuck off", and slapped me round the face. I picked her up by the throat, slammed her up against the wall and wanted her to die.

'She didn't go back to the party. But that was the end of the marriage, really. She said that it was only after that night that she decided to have a proper affair with that bloke at the party. I didn't know about it. I was very unhappy and working long hours because it was important to me to be successful at work. It was the only place I had any identity other than as a wimp. There I was respected for what I did,' he said.

Tony, who had moved into the country with his wife and children and opened a craft shop as a way of dealing with his own restlessness and crisis within the marriage, was immensely shocked when Beth told him she had gone out with another man and wanted to see him again.

'She had started a part-time job and the man was her boss. I couldn't believe it. I thought she had been happier since we moved. Now she had actually gone and done the thing I'd stopped myself from doing (I never acted on any of my attractions to women) and at a time when the marriage seemed healthy.

'I was extremely angry and upset but her affair hadn't become sexual yet, so I tried to handle it in a cool way. I tried to get her talking about it – I had always been the one who never wanted to talk – and everything came out then. She said she felt I didn't love her, or like her, and I excluded her from all I did. She said she wanted a real husband. My reaction was that that wasn't right, that wasn't fair, but underneath all the emotional turmoil I knew she was right.

'In a way it was an interesting time for me. I had to start getting behind all the things that put me together, all the conditioning from my family etc. I said one night, trying to be adult, "Okay, go out with him, I'll babysit."

'During the evening I became absolutely certain that they were making love. I flew into a rage and smashed up the furniture. She came back late and I screamed, "You've slept with him now! That's the end!" She denied it, then admitted it. I was crying. I was hurt and I was worried about what would happen to the children. I had a dream that night, which had been a recurring dream through marriage, of being in a house that was a prison. In the past I could never escape from it. That night I got out of the house and, as I stood on the path, I turned and saw the house collapse.

'I woke up next morning with an incredible feeling of relief. A million ton load was off me. I also felt shocked at my relief but it didn't last anyway. Very quickly I was back in an emotional state, rowing with my wife about what to do, who would go where.

'Looking back, the most useless thing I did was get so emotionally hysterical for so long. I'd advise anyone to try to get the emotions out and then over and done with, and avoid being self-indulgent. It was really damaging, I think, to have rows like that with Beth when the children were around. That still worries me now.'

Quite a few men were aware of feeling relief when their wives admitted to affairs because they already wanted to get themselves out from what had become an impasse. Neal, the ebullient artist who had married the young woman who was anorexic, had decided to leave her but planned to wait until she had finished the therapy she was currently undergoing.

'I'm sure she knew I was going to leave her. We both kept terribly busy and we were both desperate to entertain a lot, so that we wouldn't be alone together. We didn't argue because there was no point, and we slept separately.

'Then I got home one night and I could tell something had happened. She looked softer and more fragile. She had gone to bed with the man who was putting the greenhouse in our garden and it was the first purely physical sexual experience she had ever had. She fell in love with him. It was like having a sixteen-year-old in the house. She was coming alive and there was a wonderful beauty in that – it hit me too, the beauty of it. The affair went on for months. I thought all this might in fact be part of the cure but she became colder and colder and angrier towards me. So when I did leave, there was no sympathy between us at all. I was frozen out. But I shall never forget the relief.'

Lew's backache had disappeared some months after his unwilling capitulation into marriage but his and Judy's mutual frustrations had persisted. Judy had very quickly wanted a baby and Lew, reluctant because he did not feel mature enough, gave in again. In fact he was very happy with his daughter when she was born. Judy carried on working as an interior designer and they both shared her care.

'But Judy and I were terribly frustrated with each other. I felt I was superior intellectually and got annoyed at what I saw as Judy basically being rather stupid about things. She felt she was always being put upon by me. I always wanted to be right and what she did was wrong. I was bored by her. I had been to a public school and was indoctrinated to consider women second class men. She got into the women's movement in a big way and let me know it.

'Altogether we were both aware nothing was going right and we just decided to stay together as harmoniously as we could until our daughter was older, so it would be less damaging to her. She was about two then. I became more and more confused, guilty and depressed. I felt very much exploited by Judy and she felt exploited by me.

'She refused to recognise that someone has to take responsibility for certain things in life, like accounts. For all her talk of equality, she didn't even recognise there was a job to be done. She resented the fact that she felt she had to cook the meals – but if I said don't, she felt put down. It was a bizarre charade. We both resented the fact that certain things we each felt as important were regarded as boring and unnecessary by the other.

'Sex was on and off. She had another man by then but I didn't know. When she did finally tell me, I felt slightly relieved, because it made it easier just to rub along. I didn't realise how much she wanted to be with him permanently then. It must have been hard for her. I also started to assuage my frustrations elsewhere but nothing ever developed.'

Scriptwriter Morris, who is so self-deprecating about his behaviour as husband and lover, was also self-deprecating about his reaction to his wife Alice's affair.

'In the early days of our marriage, I wasn't making it in my career in the way I had expected. I feared I wasn't going to make it at all and more and more I withdrew and hid in my study, pretending I was writing. She saw what was happening and went seeking another protector, because she too feared she wasn't going to make it. She was an illustrator. This was two years after marriage, and I caught them in bed.

'I was shattered because of my own basic psychological problems, which included fear of inadequacy, particularly male and sexual. (I was weedy and sickly as a child and never gained my father's approval, who didn't think it likely I'd grow up to be a man amongst men.)

'So, here was proof of my inadequacy! Very painful, very traumatic, and very revealing, although I didn't see that at the time. Alice went off with the man, but the affair finished and she had nowhere to go, so she came back. And I took her back, because it showed me in a good light and gave me a big stick to beat her with, i.e. her guilt. I was very skilled at pressing guilt buttons. To keep the peace, she went along with it.

'I thought I loved her. But it was easy for me. I had, metaphorically, a punching bag and she was dutiful. We both had one-night stands, to prove how hip we were, and I felt hurt about hers but terribly surprised if she felt hurt by mine.

'When our son was born, she wanted to move to the country but I wanted to be in town, so in town we were. I bullied and browbeat her mercilessly. I could be very sarcastic. My father had been that way with me, so I became an abuser too.

'I was smugly content with how everything was going. It was my wife who was miserable and hid it. We were living a financially precarious life, which I found exhilarating and she found terrifying. But we both had a lot of fun with the baby. I thought I was great, bathing him, but at night it wasn't *me* who got up.

'I still had my double standards. I had quite a serious affair with a neighbourhood woman but it was a mixture of fear and responsibility that kept me from leaving my wife so that stopped. Also, she had a child and I felt I would rather father mine than hers.

'In fact I became very happy and contented. We were both doing well at work and we connected in positive ways through our son, who was lovely, cheerful and outgoing and who managed to avoid being twisted. (God knows how the product of two neurotic nutcases could be so laid back and easygoing.)

'We did have rows, which she hated. I'd end them by walking out of the room, so I could have the last word, leaving her shaking with frustration, but we kept them from our son. When he was twelve, we finally decided to move to the country. We chose a house and were about to sell up when she suddenly admitted that she couldn't go. She had been having an affair with a certain man for the last few years and now found she couldn't bear to leave him.

'I didn't know. I had ignored all the signs and had chosen to accept her explanations of why he was around. She had used to say I didn't trust her, so I had stopped laying on the guilt, and I had also become monogamous myself.

'I felt devastated because this time this was something very serious which had gone on for a long time. Sadly for her, the boyfriend had taken up with another woman, despairing that Alice would ever leave me. She was desperate to get him back. I moved out to a cold bedsitter, where she would ring me three times a day to tell me the latest of her boyfriend and reproach me for fifteen years of misery. I felt hard done by and would strike back by trying to press the guilt buttons again. But she had armour against that now – raw hostility. I started by arguing, then shut up and let her get on with it.'

## The other woman

Men are thought to have affairs more lightly than women. But for two married men, suddenly meeting someone to whom they felt attractive and by whom they were loved was a fundamental shock, and they didn't know how to handle it. They were in relationships where love and affection seemed either a rare or an unexperienced commodity but they certainly hadn't been looking for any way out. They both felt a desperate sense of conflict.

Dan had been derided by his widowed mother as a child and then married a woman who had as little conception as he did at the time that love was supposed to be about warm feelings and feeling good. As he said, 'You just got on with it, where I came from.' Then he met a woman at work whom it took him some months to realise felt very fond of him indeed.

'She was so loving and just thought I was marvellous. I was the one who was swept off my feet. I didn't know anyone could feel that way, let alone feel it about me. I became deeply attached to her and couldn't give her up. I didn't know what to do. Then my wife found out and started divorce proceedings at once. It was a terrible time. The girl died, in fact, two months before the divorce came through, so I was left with neither my family nor my prize.'

Philip, who had married when he was still very sexually inexperienced felt the relationship could have worked if he had had warmth, help, affection and love. 'I didn't get it, at the start or later. We were both virgins but she had slightly more experience than I, yet, on our wedding night, she didn't even want to make love. I felt our relationship, which was good non-sexually, would take time, and I wanted to give it time. But after six months it became clear that her chief aim was children.

'I felt it was too soon but she was determined. To my dismay, when our daughter was born, the child was withdrawn from me, so to speak, because everything I did was likely to be wrong. Her mother-in-law came between us too and I felt emotionally isolated.

'The girl I met was a friend of a friend. The attraction was instant and mutual and it was the best and happiest sexual relationship I have ever had as it was all so intense at the time.

'I knew I wanted an affair with her before it got that far and it preyed on my mind, so I went to see a psychiatrist where, for the first time, I was able to let my feelings out and talk. He was a very wise man. He said, "You have no choice, you will have the affair and your marriage may not survive, but it will if there is enough respect and love. If you don't have the affair, you'll have it in your head forever." I should have got all that sort of thing done before marriage, of course.

'I told my wife what the psychiatrist had said and suggested I leave home, till I got the affair out of my system. I was very unhappy, uncertain and unsettled. I went and saw her and our daughter a few times and then learned that, without saying anything, she had started divorce proceedings.

'I still feel the marriage could have worked if my wife and I had been strong enough to handle the emotional upheaval of my affair. I didn't feel I had been misunderstood, but that there had been such a lack of forgiveness and human warmth on her part. I know now how it feels to be ditched by someone you love and, though I felt cut up for a long time, I managed to ride above that, and there are very warm feelings now.

'My wife had in fact found an innocent letter from the girl before anything started and instantly said, "We must tell your parents". I feel I was divorced not for having an affair, but for wanting one.'

Pete, who had hit his wife after the fateful New Year's Eve party, had also been attracted to a girl who made him aware for the first time of what was missing in his marriage.

'I was feeling so miserable, so unhappy about my relationship with Pam which was all abuse and hurt feelings. I met Jill at a college where I was going for some day-release courses. She was seventeen, I was twenty-three, had been married for three years and had two sons. I talked to Jill at a college do and then gave her a lift home one night and and talked to her for two hours outside her house. My first good feeling was that I actually *could* talk to her.

'She was lovely. She stroked *me* and I found that attractive. I took her out over a few months. There was never any sex but I was in love with her. I wanted to be honest with her. So finally I told her I was married and wouldn't leave my children. I wanted to leave Pam. I knew now there could be something else in life, something that made me feel better than I was. But when I told Jill, it hurt us both so much that I felt dreadful guilt. I decided never to play around again, because it caused so much hurt on both sides.

'But then I desperately wanted the relationship with Pam to work, to be like it was with Jill. We did manage to have some good times. But if you abuse each other like we did, you can't get close again.

'Pam had an affair before the one we split up over. The man was married with three kids and wouldn't leave his wife. I didn't want the marriage to break up, although it hurt me to see how much she loved that man. So I told her about Jill and said I knew how she felt.

'She went crazy. She wouldn't believe it hadn't been sexual. It was as if she hadn't had an affair and I had. She was just malicious about it and blamed everything that had gone wrong in our marriage on me. It was all about who was blaming who, not about how badly we had been hurt.'

Jay, who had repressed all his grief about his stillborn baby, felt that at a particular point he deliberately looked for an affair. His feelings were still pent up at that stage and, to add to those, he was experiencing extreme anxiety about his work. He was trying to write an important paper on education and couldn't get himself together at all.

'I wanted to work in the evenings because of my guilt at not achieving. But I also felt guilty about leaving Shelley alone. So I would stay with Shelley but we just watched TV without communicating. I couldn't communicate because I was feeling so guilty about not working and so screwed up in myself by that stage. So I gave her nothing anyway and I know she was terribly unhappy.

'She had had enough when Vicky was a year old. She took Vicky to see her mother in Canada. I couldn't go because of work. But as soon as she left I went straight down the tube.

'I felt I desperately needed to be with someone. I was getting buried and things were getting blacker and blacker. I remembered a woman I had met through work and dropped around to see her. We ended up having an affair for two weeks while Shelley was away.

'I felt I was making someone happy for a change (I knew I had been making Shelley very unhappy) and that was very liberating. I ended the affair just before Shelley came back. I still wanted the good feelings but I was a husband and a father. I was a real mess.

'By the time Shelley came back, I was crazy, irrational and depressed. I'd experienced openness in the affair and I wanted that, I didn't want to hide things anymore. So I instantly told Shelley of the affair. I irrationally hoped that by wanting openness, lightness and freedom within our relationship, I'd get it at once.

'Shelley was literally just back, jetlagged and everything. Of course she was very upset and crying. She kept saying, "You have to choose," and I remember thinking, puzzled, "but I've already chosen" – her, Shelley. I walked out at midnight, I couldn't take anymore.

'I think Shelley had had enough and wanted out. She says she thinks I wanted out but I can't see that, because Vicky meant so much to me. But I remember the incredible freedom I felt when I left the house – to be out in the darkness away from the house, the pressure.

'Then I started feeling crunching anxiety until I became virtually non-functional. Effectively the marriage ended then, though we tried recon-ciliation. I had been diagnosed as clinically depressed by that time and was having therapy and I was really just camping at our house, giving masses of attention to Vicky. She was the one sane point in my life.'

Only two men who had serious affairs over which their marriages broke up say they felt no guilt about why they started them or about how their wives would feel.

Charles, the businessman who said his marriage lacked chemistry or communication, has a complete blank about quite how his first affair started. He knew he was being driven by a need for sex and for com-panionship and the affair, once started, ended up lasting two years. 'We used to see each other about twice a week. We would have lunch and spend the afternoons together. I didn't reason out what I was doing or why. In the end, I couldn't take the complications workwise, so I said it had to stop. Also, I was nervous of our being seen.

'She wasn't my type sexually either, although I hadn't yet discovered who was. I had a couple of short affairs and then I met Maria. She too was married and had two children.

'We were very physically attracted to each other. She was a very fun person. She had a need to make everything exciting for herself and in so doing she made them exciting for the people she was with. She made sex exciting. She and I were very well adjusted.

'We spent a lot of time together. I would see her for half days but we also managed whole weekends and holidays, although I don't remember how I ever explained that to Deborah! We went abroad lots of times. Maria's relationship with her husband was odd. He may have had affairs too, but anyway, she didn't find it difficult to make excuses for herself.

'At the time it never came up whether we wanted to marry. Neither of us wanted to break our marriages and we were both devoted to our children. In some ways we found it ideal.

'With Deborah, the sex had gone out of our marriage. I wasn't approaching her sexually any more but she wasn't approaching me either. She did complain sometimes but I think she was pleased it was out of the way. She is very scared of her own emotions and sex, very threatened by her own sexual feelings. So I think she just nominally complained.

'I didn't feel at all guilty at that stage. I used to feel she had it coming to her. She was neglecting the house and not supporting my career. I didn't think that she appreciated the life I was able to give her through the exacting and gruelling work I had to do – there was the lovely house, expensive holidays, private schools for the children. She didn't earn much herself as a nursery school teacher. I was always there in the evenings, anyway, and we did lots of things with the children.

'I never rationalised any of what was happening. It was just happening. I didn't think, "this is a good solution", although I wish it could have gone on like that.

'But Maria rang me one morning and said she had told her husband about us. I kept calm but I thought, how stupid. Apparently her husband had confessed an affair and she had retaliated with me. The next thing was that they split up and got divorced. (We both sacrificed a lot in all this – I a beautiful house in town and she a lovely mansion in the country. She bought a flat down there.) Then the pressure started for me to leave Deborah for her. The pressure was terrible for me. In the end I told Deborah about Maria because I couldn't go on living with the situation. Maria was on her own with two children now. It had ceased to be so nice and easy.

'Deborah said she couldn't believe it at the time. I feel she had unconsciously known for years and wasn't dissatisfied because it left her alone, yet didn't take away from the family. When I told her, however, she had to let it into her consciousness.

'There was terrible tension in the house but I moved into the spare room and that helped, because I get up early and was away before the house was up. I think, in retrospect, that Deborah acted extremely maturely about it all. We told the children about Maria. They took it fairly calmly, I think, I don't remember. Then we went to therapy.'

Dave, a company biochemist, had felt nothing was left in his marriage to Anthea. They had four children but had ceased to communicate and shared no interests. He was unhappy but had no thought to leave the marriage. He just thought that was what marriage was like.

'Then there was a party at work. I got drunk and had a one-night stand with a secretary. I would never have done that normally but it did change me. I was with colleagues, having fun. I got a taste for something more lively and exciting in life.

'During our marriage, Anthea and I had hardly ever socialised, except with her family. We never gave dinner parties or anything like that. My wife didn't know of the one-night stand and things just went on as before. Then, six months later, there was another party and another one-nighter. I did like the girls concerned but I shut off the possibility of anything more with them because, after all, in the cold light of day, I was married. I did not feel regret about any of it, which perhaps I ought have.

'It didn't happen again for quite a long time, though I innocently used to take one girl out to lunch. Finding it interesting talking to other people made my interest in home even less.

'I started staying after work and drinking with colleagues and sometimes did not even get home until 1.30 in the morning, if we went for a meal. Anthea didn't like that. She said I worked too much or was out with the boys and she was lonely. I said she wasn't interested in anything I did. I was very depressed and felt impossibly trapped.'

He had by then made up his mind that he would leave Anthea when his youngest child, then twelve, was old enough. Then, at yet another party, he met another girl with whom he stayed the night and did start a relationship.

'I was so depressed about my life by then that I told my wife about her. She went berserk. She screamed and howled and threw books at me. She wanted me to give up the relationship but I wouldn't. I didn't give a damn about her feelings to be honest. It had all gone.

'We both tried to hide the fact that something was wrong from the children but they knew something was going on. They would creep downstairs at night to hear what we were saying. My relationship with the girl wasn't serious but I needed her and some nights I didn't come home. I told Anthea I was at conferences and she told that to the children, but she knew really where I was, I'm sure.

'I realised I was hurting the children because they were so confused. I knew I was doing them no good but at that point I didn't have the guts to pull out.'

He even remembers in his own mind blaming Anthea for much that had happened to him, for creating what he saw as a stultifying marriage, obliging him to seek stimulation and expression outside it. The genuine affection he knew she felt towards him he had long ceased to be able to return. If there was any guilt or sense of loss, it was overridden by despair and blame. At that point he had no wish to save the marriage, although he did have a terror of the upheaval that leaving it would cause.

Not all men wanted their marriages to end despite affairs, their own or their wives'. It seemed however that in each case, and regardless of who was the 'guilty' party, the affair signalled crunch point for one or other. Because the affairs were symptoms rather than causes of the marriage breakdown, both partners had perhaps already experienced deep hurt, a hurt which was for one of them, at least, too deep to want to try and heal.

# ═══4═══
# The break

Breaking up a marriage is sometimes sudden, sometimes drawn out, but always immediately physically as well as emotionally traumatic for one partner. Usually that partner is the man. However much sharing of responsibility there is in a marriage, it is more often the woman who keeps the invisible wheels of the home machinery turning; so many men are trying to adapt to being solely responsible for their own needs while also trying to cope with guilt and fear over the children's feelings and futures, and intense personal feelings of failure and loss.

Traditionally, too, men tend not to have intimate friendships in the way that women do. It is women who more often discuss and support each others' marital relationships while men's connection with other men depends more on common interests outside of themselves.

Whether this difference is social, psychological or biologically based, it ceases to be solely of academic interest when men split up from their wives. Often they flounder badly through failing to find emotional support or their inability to make full use of what is offered to them. As one man said: 'I could have talked to my parents or my brother but I felt it was silly. When people talk to me of their private problems, I can't really feel what they are going through. So I feel it's better to keep these things to yourself. I suppose it is my paranoia that my brother wouldn't be interested, rather than knowing that he wasn't.'

Some men found that they had no friends after the marriage was over, either because the marriage itself was insular or because they felt mutual friends had taken the side of their wives. Or, even if other couples had not taken sides, it only compounded problems for some men if they stayed friendly with people whom the wife felt she had a greater 'right' to.

Interestingly, to me, no one stressed the physical discomforts and difficulties of managing alone, whatever their financial circumstances and however much they had been shielded from the domestic responsibilities of home – possibly because all recalled the emotional anguish as so catastrophic.

As it so happened that none of the men I spoke to left their wives to live with another woman, all therefore had to find their own ways of dealing, suddenly, with life without their partner. The painful reactions and feelings experienced were sometimes as strong for men who had not had children as for those who had.

Laurie, for instance, who had married so quickly after his mother's death, re-experienced that same sense of tumultuous and irreplaceable loss when his wife Carol chose to leave him. The two events were unconsciously closely connected.

He had had no idea that Carol was even less than happy, as they had never discussed deeper emotional needs. It was a complete shock when one day she phoned him at work and said: 'We've something serious to talk about. I'll meet you at 5 p.m.' In the pub near his office, she told him that she was leaving. He still doesn't know, because he didn't ask, why she felt she had to tell him outside of the house.

'It was an appalling shock – just like my mother's death all over again. She explained that she felt unfulfilled and that there was nowhere for the marriage to go, but that didn't make sense to me at the time. It seemed so pie in the sky, so unrealistic and romantic. She wanted to experience life, she said. I was very depressed by it all.

'She had had a brief affair with someone, it seemed, but she was adamant that that was a symptom rather than a cause. I was numb. I went to the house, gathered up some things and went to stay with my sister for two weeks, while Carol moved out.

'My sister and an old male schoolfriend of mine tried to give me sympathy and support. But I was at great pains that they shouldn't see Carol as the villain of the piece. I didn't pour my heart out because I didn't know my heart at the time, although I appreciated that they wanted to help. I could only allow myself to explore what Carol wasn't getting from the marriage. It didn't even occur to me that I wasn't getting certain things I needed either. I now know everyone has needs and you shouldn't ignore them.

'I couldn't face moving back to the house and started to do odd things. I camped out in the country and lived hand to mouth. I drank and took lots of tranquillisers. I was quite a mess for two or three months – I'd gone awol from work but afterwards I did get my job back.

'Looking back, I couldn't cope emotionally at all. I was full of excuses for Carol but at the same time I felt terrible pain and when I felt the pain, I drank and got philosophical about it all.

'I must have felt anger but it was all carefully suppressed and rationalised away. I couldn't abide the thought that Carol was blameworthy, and didn't consider that I was. I didn't look at myself and say, "Where did *you* fail?" I accepted the fiction and that was that.'

Pam also initiated the end of her marriage to Pete with a phone call. 'She rang me at work,' he said, 'and told me that when I got home that night we had to talk about Roger – the man she had been kissing at the New Year's Eve party. I went home straight away. We had often used to go out with Roger and his wife and I had felt some suspicions but I had said nothing because she would call me stupid and possessive and we'd row.

'Pam told me she and Roger had something going. It was as if she was saying, "There's a problem, what shall I do?" I told her I was going to leave her. I wasn't prepared to take any more.

'I just left and went to my parents' place. She burst into tears and begged me not to go. That really moved me – that she was crying over *me* – but I said it was no good. I just wanted to get away. Roger lived opposite me. For months Pam had refused to shut the front room curtains at night and now I realised that it was so that they could see each other. I felt, "I can't live here any more and look at those curtains!"

'I was so upset. At my mum's I didn't know what to do. All of us were upset. I was so mixed up. I didn't know if I was just making a gesture and it would all be all right. I didn't know what to do.

'I rang Pam the next day. She said Roger had also told his wife and he was leaving her. I went to see him that night and told him he was scum. He moved in four days after I left.

'It's all very confused. I know I came to see the children every Sunday but I don't remember how I felt. You don't know what to do with yourself. The whole structure I had built around my life had gone. I didn't want to go home from work but I couldn't stay late at work either – I couldn't bear to stay in any one place too long. I drank myself into oblivion. I used to keep saying "I don't want to be here anymore" and leave wherever I was.

'I felt all my goals had gone and I'd failed. I felt so bad I couldn't think, let alone make any decision, about the kids and the house. All I could think was "I'm a fuck up". I just didn't know what I was going to do.

'I was so afraid of the unknown. I don't blame Pam for crying when I left. At that moment she didn't know what would happen to her either. I used to think, "What am I going to do at nights? How will I get through them?" I had no real friends. My parents tried to be supportive but saying

Pam was a bitch and that I was better off without her wasn't what I needed. I needed to feel better about me. I needed them to say, "We love you, son". That would have been supportive.'

Some other men also said it didn't help to hear friends and family criticising or condemning their wives. They felt driven to defend them (in a way that, perhaps, women in the same position don't) and, in a way, were defending themselves – they had, after all, chosen to be married to the person who was then receiving such short shrift from other quarters. As one said: 'I found myself getting protective about her if they said anything negative.' Another: 'I knew they were trying to be nice but I didn't want to hear what they were saying.' Certainly they still loved their wives but, in feeling forced onto the defensive, they may not have been able to articulate their hurt. As Pete found, he needed to feel better about *himself*.

Unlike Pete and Laurie, most of the men I spoke to found the ending of their marriage was not a sudden shock, out of the blue. They knew it was on a downhill spiral but neither they nor their partner could bear or dare to confront the enormity of what that meant. As one man said: 'Why did it continue? There's a certain disbelief about the pain which stops one realising there's an option to stop it. And habits get set up. The separation gets bigger and bigger, the distance grows but if no revelation big enough happens, or there's no courage to examine the situation properly, you just carry on. Then something happens that you can't ignore any more, the whole house of cards comes down and you are totally unequipped to deal with it.'

But men in marriages which had been cranking painfully to a halt, in which crisis *had* been acknowledged and attempts made to solve it by trial separations, felt no less desperate and disoriented when the inevitable partings came. The separations led to no changes in the relationship and thus didn't help them to ease back into their marriages as hoped. But, because the separations were intrinsically temporary, they did not act as a means of easing them out of their marriages either. As one marriage guidance expert commented, it can be harder to go back to a marriage after separation, if no help has been sought for problems during the break; and the unfounded expectation that all will suddenly be better and different may compound the feelings of frustration and failure when the opposite ensues.

Jeff, the architect, and his wife Kay had been fighting constantly for some months before Kay suggested that they try separating for a while, to see if that helped. 'I had never heard of such an idea,' he said, 'and resisted it strongly. But then, after a while, I encouraged it because things were so awful.' He worked from home, so they arranged that they would take it in turns to leave for a couple of months and stay with friends while the other looked after the children.

'When I was away, all I felt was lonely and miserable. I wanted us to be together again and yet, when we were, we had even more fights than before. I didn't know whether it was better to stay or try leaving for a while again. It was a dreadful time, I kept thinking, should I, shouldn't I, what will it achieve? Eventually I took a lease on a small office and camped there too.

'I saw the children whenever I wanted but I was so lonely. Kay and I both saw ourselves as not sure where to go with the marriage. I stayed with her one night and she asked me to come back (she says I asked her), so once again I did. Then a disastrous holiday together made us agree we had to separate for good.

'I moved back to the office. The feelings of loneliness and desperation were even more strong and this time it wasn't going to end. I couldn't find any positive feelings about making a fresh start because I had been at this point before. Then I had at least hope. Now I had nothing. I remember only the worry about the children and confusion. I knew I had to learn to live with myself and didn't just want to fill up my time because I was lonely. But I found myself doing anything just to have contact with other people all the time.'

Frank also tried trial separation as a last resort. He now believes that he and Sarah had never communicated properly during their marriage and had ignored all the bad signs, including a very unsatisfactory sex life, while the relationship descended downhill.

'It had been a slow deterioration right from the start,' he said, 'but the real crunch came two years before we separated. That is when it came out in the open that we had a problem. We had stopped having any sex, it just happened, and we were arguing incessantly. The children knew what was happening and that worried me. The arguments always seemed to happen when the children were around.'

They talked about what to do and tried various kinds of therapy, which, he says, almost worked at one point. 'But then I ran out of ideas about what to do and left for a month. I just had to get away, I couldn't stand it, but I didn't think anything positive would happen,' he said. He saw the children regularly and then moved back home, only to try another separation later. 'But I realised that being away didn't help to solve any problems as far as keeping our marriage going, so I decided to leave for good.

'I wanted it to be a planned departure. I wanted to sort out the financial problems, maintenance, finish jobs on the house. We sorted it out between us but not very amicably. Sarah didn't try to persuade me to stay.

'Leaving home for good was such an upheaval. My daughter, who was eight, said: "You're not getting divorced, are you?" and I said no and felt guilty. She must have been upset but she didn't show it. It was probably harder for the little boy – he was much younger and probably had no idea what was going on. Every time I saw them they would say, "Are you coming back?" and that was very upsetting. There is still a corner of that now, five years later. I still haven't come to terms with it.

'I feel I've let them down and given them a very bad start. On the other hand I don't regret doing it. Very selfish, isn't it?

'When I finally decided to leave, it was when everything I did seemed to be wrong and didn't please my wife. My daughter did actually once say it might be better for them if I left. It was that bad for the children.

'Sarah and I argued about whether to tell them the truth about why I kept not being there. She didn't want to and I regret giving in on that. We used to say I was away on work etc. But I think children are more adaptable than adults and can cope if they know what's going on.

'My parents used to fight and pretend it was play-acting. But I knew they were fighting! I think it is very belittling to children to lie to them.' (Men whose children were old enough to understand at least something did feel happier about the effects on them of the break-up if they had managed to be truthful.)

'I moved into a bedsit and felt very disoriented. I had no close friends. If I hadn't had my job, I would have cracked up. But that at least was familiar territory. At least one part of my life was normal.

'I had started an affair shortly before I left, although that was not the cause of my leaving. It foundered pretty quickly but having had it boosted my morale. My self-confidence had had a puff when it needed it. My self-esteem had got so low during the break-up that it seemed hard to believe anyone could love me at all, even for a short time.'

Lew was also suffering from extremely low morale by the time he and Judy, who were sitting their unsatisfactory marriage out as long as they could for the sake of their daughter, decided to separate. Grace, their daughter, was then eight, and it was Judy who took the initiative to end the marriage. Lew said: 'By that time I was so depressed about myself and feeling so incompetent that I couldn't have made any decisions. I had thought I would have to be the one to sort things out and take the responsibility for making the living arrangements and so on. That kind of thing tended to be left to me but I wasn't capable at the time of doing it either. However, Judy was much more of a mind to leave than I had realised and did take the initiative when her lover had left his wife.

'We told Grace what it would mean in terms of the pattern of her life but in many ways that didn't change very much. Judy and Martin, the lover, got a place very close by, so I saw my daughter almost daily. She popped round or stayed and I also went to their house. I think Martin found that difficult, though I didn't. I had always been able to cook, so nothing much changed at my house except that the garden went to pot. Judy had liked doing all that.' He and Judy even managed to maintain many of their mutual friends without dissension.

While on the surface, therefore, nothing much changed, as Lew put it, and he did not have to cope with the physical and emotional upheaval of moving or seeing significantly less of his daughter and friends, he was in severe emotional crisis, unable to come to terms with what he saw as all his personal failures, which a failed marriage had thrown fully into focus. That he had to cope with alone. As he said, 'Despite the fact that I wasn't physically alienated, I couldn't talk to friends about my problems and insecurities because I was the one who was unwilling to talk or allow that kind of closeness. I don't find it easy to talk about me. I had to sort myself out and that took a couple of very painful years, as I had lost all faith in myself.'

For Tony, the painful process of personal re-evaluation was equally long. Tony had smashed up the furniture after Beth began her affair and had numerous hysterical scenes with her over splitting up, which he regrets because of the children. The relief he had felt when they had agreed to part was not long-lasting. 'Beth wouldn't change her mind and wanted the marriage to end. Between rows we had to work out what would happen to the house and who would go where. At one point she was going to move in with her boyfriend and I was going to stay in the house with the children. I think I could have handled it but I found the practicalities daunting at the time.

'The decision took about three months to make. Meanwhile we had mentally split the house in two and were living fairly separate lives. We were both worried about the children and how to deal with things best for them. Eventually we agreed I would leave, her man would buy my half of the house and the children would stay there. I couldn't allow a suggestion of Beth's that she take the children to his house to live. It felt as though I would be handing my children over and I couldn't do it.

'The children were aware that something was happening. They were ten and eight. The elder, the boy, was confused and said, "Are you still my dad?" and it was the little girl who said, "Of course he's our dad. He always will be." '

Tony moved into rooms in the next town and became very unsociable and introverted, 'trying to come to an understanding of why I was where I was. But I was lucky to have a close man and a woman friend who helped me a lot,' he said. All the same, it took him two years, like Lew, to stop questioning and condemning himself and to come to terms with his past and his future, and to deal with his guilt and worry over the children's feelings.

Most men who did not involve their children fully and openly in the decisions that were being made about separation, if the children were old enough to understand, said, years on, that that was what they regretted most about their handling of the break-up. Often they felt later that their failure to establish an atmosphere of openness and trust at the outset made it difficult for their children to reveal, directly, their worries and insecurities during the circumscribed times that they met thereafter. Conversely, those men whose children were told the truth, without parental bitterness intruding, and reassured about what it meant for themselves, specifically recalled that as something they were very relieved and glad they had done, however difficult and painful at the time.

Dave, one of the two men who felt no guilt over affairs, had only stayed in his marriage because of the children. But when his unhappiness had driven him to the point where he had resorted to drinking and often not coming home, he knew he was doing them more harm than good. He didn't know what to do or how to do it and was on the point of a nervous breakdown. So when indecision finally tipped into decision, he felt a blind need to act at once, seeing no way, in his emotional state by that time, to soften his children's pain.

'I was hardly functioning any more when I talked to my brother – we were very close – and asked what he thought I should do. He said: "You'll have to leave". I needed the push to go and he gave it to me. He came home with me and waited in the car, while I went in to pack a suitcase. I thought I'd get my exit ready first, before confronting Anthea with my decision. But she came upstairs, saw what I was doing and was so enraged and upset that she started opening all the drawers and cupboards and just throwing everything on the floor.

'I went on packing the suitcase. She kept throwing herself at me and seizing my arms until finally I had to say I would hit her if she didn't stop. She stopped. I would hate to go through a scene like that again ever. Then I went downstairs to the four children (the eldest was seventeen, the youngest was twelve). I told them Anthea and I couldn't live together any more, that I had to leave but I would be in contact with them very soon.

'They all burst into tears. The youngest came rushing out after me, calling me. I didn't turn round. I felt terrible. I had let those children down so much, but I had made up my mind and felt I had to do it.

'I stayed at friends' houses, hotels. I didn't feel liberated. I felt diabolical. In the end I slept on my brother's sofa for six months.'

Charles only told his wife Deborah about Maria, the woman with whom he had been having an intense relationship for some years, when the pressure from Maria on him to leave his wife became too much to bear.

'We then told the children – the youngest was thirteen. I think I told them that I had met someone I loved very much and that it was possible to love two people in different ways. I think I said to Deborah I'd like to keep both her and Maria, say, stay with Maria two nights a week. But neither she nor Maria would wear it, of course!

'The tension in the house was bad, though Deborah and I had started seeing some marriage guidance people, and once the children even came too. I was terrified the children were going to turn against me and reject me. They were actually urging me to leave. But it wasn't because they wanted me out of the way. They were very co-operative and helped me move. I think they felt it would be better for their mother and they sensed that they wouldn't be losing me, that I was deeply attached to them.

'I was in terrible dilemma about moving. Maria wanted me to move in with her but I didn't want to, because I didn't feel the children could accept that and I would lose them. So I moved into a poky little flat of my own. It was supposed to be a thinking time for me, till I had decided whether I wanted Deborah or Maria. I was pulled all ways and felt very bad.'

Many men did experience relief as well as disorientation but that feeling was naturally more easily accessible to those who didn't have children. Neal knew he wanted to leave his wife, who had had anorexia, but he was still nervous of making the actual physical break.

'I didn't want to leave my home, my space, and go out into that wild floating population with no roots, no address. But finally I did leave and go and stay in a friend's house.

'And then I felt born again! I shall never forget the relief, the light-heartedness, the peace, centred in my being. I suddenly had all my energy back.

'I lived out of suitcases for two years and loved it. I was uncluttered by possessions. It seemed to me our possessions had replaced something more fundamental we couldn't achieve. I think so many marriages do that. I don't care if my marriage isn't rich next time. But it must be rich emotionally, and deep, and I'm prepared to work very hard to have that.'

When Angus, also childless, decided to take account of his own needs and feelings and separate from his manic-depressive wife Claire, he felt Neal's sense of freedom and relief, yet fighting against that was an inability to shed his sense of responsibility for and connection to Claire.

'When she left, I felt absolutely liberated,' he recalls, 'but there was also a lot of worry, although no guilt. Sometimes late at night she would phone me and wail. She wanted to come back. I felt dreadful. I knew I couldn't have her back and retain my sanity but I felt so impotent.

'She still haunts me even now and I sometimes have bad dreams about her. I felt I hadn't freed myself from her as a problem because, if she rang or called round, I couldn't throw her out. I felt put upon.

'She could be so unreasonable, it seemed to me. She moved out before taking her things and I worked like buggery packing all her stuff up very carefully so it wouldn't break. She didn't want me to move her, she wanted a friend of hers to do it. So I helped him load up his van and then Claire said I should pay him for doing it! I felt it was up to her and was very angry and resentful.

'Once we had officially separated, I felt a bereavement. That is, there was definitely something missing in my life, despite the relief, and I imagined it as much like a bereavement. I sold the house and, on the last day, I was hoovering the landing preparatory to leaving and I started weeping my eyes out. I had a terrible feeling of emptiness, despite all the horrific times.'

Donald, who had the horror of suburbia and routine existence, expected to feel relieved when his wife decided to leave him. But he also felt continuing responsibility. 'We had had a very traumatic last six months, with all the emotional frustration and lack of communication, and I couldn't cope.

'But Joanna left with the idea of wanting me to want her back. It dawned on her very quickly that I didn't want to be married to her any more. I felt very hard about saying no. The image of her whole life had been shattered and all I could do that would help her was to have her back. But I couldn't do that. I remained extremely wretched until she got involved with someone else.'

For his own part, he suddenly found he was isolated. 'After my marriage, I didn't have any friends,' he said. 'I think, historically, men are more involved with work and know people through work, or through sport, if they do it. But they are acquaintances.

'It is women who have the friends, who organise the family parties etc.

Usually it is their friends plus the husbands, rather than the husband's friends plus the wives. At the time you see them as shared friends but when you split up, yes, they are quite clearly the wife's friends.

'I tend to talk more easily to women anyway, and you don't usually have separate friends when you are married. Women can be friends with other women, in a way that men can't with men, because there isn't that same male competitiveness. I think that, in a very deep-rooted way, men are more threatened by other men.'

Most men I spoke to talked, if they had anyone to talk to at all, to women rather than men. They had never established the kind of relationship where intimacies could be broached with the men they did consider as reasonably close friends. Two who did claim they talked to men seemed to talk mainly about the practicalities of their situation rather than the emotional consequences of attachment.

The emotional consequences included a strong if brief desire, for two of the men at least, to return to the wives that they had wanted so desperately to leave. Neal, who remembers with such clarity his feeling of being reborn once he had left his wife, also recalls feeling nostalgia.

'After I left, she suddenly seemed appealing to me, but I didn't do anything about it. When the decree nisi was granted, I saw her for the first time in a year. I took her out to lunch and asked if she really wanted to go through with the decree absolute. I did want to go back in a way, for the companionship, comfort and the good things we had had. I was working very hard and my whole life seemed hard. I thought I was sexually wiser and that she was too. I wasn't much more attracted to her sexually than I had ever been but my fleeting relationships since hadn't been good and I didn't necessarily think I'd find better.

'But I was also very relieved when she didn't want a reconciliation. I didn't, either, want to lose my freedom.'

Dave, at whose departure from the house there had been such scenes of screaming and crying, later had to see his wife to sort out joint affairs. 'We met at the house and we sort of re-started the relationship. Even sex, although I had ceased to want sex with Anthea years ago. But this time it felt different. Almost like a one-night stand! I thought that was probably because there was no commitment on my part.

'But I did feel we might even end up back together again. Anthea was extremely keen to have me back and I felt lulled by the familiarity and safety. But it went too fast and I thought, "What am I doing? If it didn't work before, it won't work now." So I eased off and she realised what was happening. She was upset, yes, but then she started having relationships and enjoying herself and it was she who took the initiative to divorce me and is now married to someone else.'

Many men who had not wanted their marriages to break up did of course wish there could be a reconciliation, but most were realistic. Marcus, who had kept all his insecurities about his inadequacy as a person and a provider bottled up and who was terribly shocked when Rosalie called the halt, said: 'I did accuse her of not giving us enough chance afterwards, as there was so much at stake with the children. But she said she couldn't have gone backwards. I do think chances are loaded against couples who try it because it *is* a going back to old patterns usually, not a going forward.'

Dick, however, went into an emotional frenzy in his attempts to re-establish his relationship with his wife Ruth. He had known, in his heart, they weren't suited, yet carried on catching at Ruth's solutions, such as marriage, havng a baby and then moving to a bigger flat, until they mutually agreed the marriage couldn't work. It was because he was still such a reluctant father, by the time Tim was four, that Ruth suggested separation. She was frightened that Tim would feel more rejected by an absent father physically present than one he saw less often but maybe received more attention from.

It turned out to be true. Dick said: 'I saw Tim once or twice a week. When we had had him, the decision I had taken was not to have a child but to have a solution to a relationship problem. It was only after the relationship ended that I could accept that I had a child for himself. It was then that my feelings about him immediately changed. I felt he was my son.

'Because Ruth and I parted on amicable terms,and we still cared about each other, I often stayed for supper after I had seen Tim and then started staying the night. Then Ruth found that, emotionally, she couldn't handle that. But it seemed as if things were sliding back, because the pattern wasn't really broken, we were still seeing each other.

'Nothing else was happening in my life because I wasn't meeting new people. I spent all my time there with Tim. I realised for the first time the loss of "family" and Ruth and Tim had become more and more important to me.

'I had one last go at making it work.I put all my emotional energy into it, telling Ruth I wanted us to get back together and trying to come to some way of working towards that. It was the first time I had cried. Logically, I knew, there was no reason why it should have worked and it didn't. She couldn't trust that I had really changed enough and that things wouldn't slip back to how they were. She was very tight and tense with me. After months of emotional turmoil, I accepted that it was finished.'

Although a marriage that has broken up has to remain very much a live issue if there needs to be connection because of children, unconscious attachment to the partner often persists for years. One man realised, to his surprise, when I asked him, that he wouldn't like his wife to marry again because then he would feel he had 'lost' her. He has been divorced for some years and has not the slightest wish for reconciliation.

Another man, who split up from his wife eight years ago, immediately rang to ask her advice and help when he was evicted from his flat. 'It just didn't occur to me to ask anyone else,' he said, despite the fact that by then he was living with a girlfriend. A third wryly recalls driving 'home' one night, exhausted after twelve hours at work, to the house where his ex-wife and child still lived instead of to his own flat. He had left her four years previously.

But it was two childless men who mentioned that they didn't feel fully free to be themselves, even after the divorce they had both wanted.

Neal said: 'Marriage is a much more profound learning process than living together can ever be. It is so public. And going through a religious ceremony, whether religious or not, has a profound emotional effect. I felt she would remain a part of my life, as my wife, even after our divorce. Fortunately, that feeling of being inevitably bound together in some psychic way is starting to lessen now.'

The emotional strain of being the sturdy supportive one in his marriage to the very vulnerable manic-depressive Claire has had a lasting effect upon Angus. 'After we were apart I began to realise that, although I had never come near murdering her, I would only feel I was free if she were dead. Even when divorced, I felt I couldn't be free of her in my head. Five years later, a little of that is still with me,' he said. He wishes he could know that she was happy and well, and then he could let her go.

There is probably little chance of marriage break-up being untraumatic in some sense, however much it is wanted or even mutually planned. In both cases, the disorientation must still be extreme because, however clear or right the decision to part, there is likely to be unexpectedly strong emotional ambivalence. No matter how bad things were, which prompted the parting, there would also have been a great many good times too – forgotten, perhaps, in the fury of fighting, but poignantly recalled later, alone. It may take time to stop regretting or denying the love that has been lost and accept it as a once very real part of a marriage that didn't always last.

# 5
# Counselling

Twice as many more women than men seek help from marriage guidance counsellors, in the early or later stages of marital difficulties, and although more couples now also attend together, it is usually the woman who makes the approach. 'That does tell a tale and reflect the difficulty men find in asking for counselling,' said Renate Olins, director of the London Marriage Guidance Council. 'I would have expected the gap to have narrowed by now and it hasn't.'

For some people, women as well as men, unfounded images of counsellors as conventionally-minded do-gooders, determined to save a marriage at any cost, may be a put-off. Others may give up when they find that in most areas there is a waiting list (although everyone is eventually seen) or are unwilling or unable to make time to attend in the day, when more appointments are available. 'But we are not a crisis organisation,' said Renate Olins. 'Marriage guidance is a reflective process. People will see the same counsellor for one hour a week for as long as they need. And men, when they do come, are *not* more resistant than women, however unacceptable they find it initially to express their feelings.'

About half of the men I spoke to said that seeking help through marriage guidance or another sort of therapy did not even occur to them during the decline of their marriages. Some of them recalled that with surprise, as if they now felt it odd that they had not thought to explore that option, and several themselves were able, in retrospect, to isolate a certain point, well before parting, when outside assistance might have helped to re-open at least a channel of communication.

It wasn't uncommon, however, to feel that seeking help outside was an open admission of failure, a sign of weakness and inadequacy as a human being. For Marcus, already bogged down by his inability to face what he saw as his failure to provide responsibly and effectively for his family, the idea of marriage guidance was altogether too confronting.

'Rosalie asked me to go to marriage guidance and I, in ignorance, pooh-poohed it. I said, "We should be able to sort our problems out ourselves", that kind of thing. I'm so ashamed of my ignorance. I knew we were estranged but never thought we would part,' he said. It was later, too late to save his marriage, however, that he did have counselling and experienced what he can only describe as revelation.

Some men did consider or try marriage guidance only as a last desperate attempt to prevent parting, and therefore it often came at a time when one partner already had a closed mind to any kind of help. In quite a few cases, it was the wife who refused to go.

Robert, the builder, who had twice caught out his wife with other men, said that he had begged his wife for a long time to come with him to marriage guidance. She refused until finally she decided that 'she owed me that much' and said she could come that Friday. But when Robert rang the local Marriage Guidance Council, he found that the system didn't work quite like that. There was a waiting list and, when it did come to his turn, he would be offered a time, not vice versa. He reported that back and his wife at once withdrew her cooperation. 'It was that Friday or not at all, as far as she was concerned. That was as far as she was prepared to go,' he said. 'But, in all honesty, I don't think it would have helped us. I don't feel she would have gone in there and listened. If she had heard something she didn't like, she'd have just walked out.'

Robert kept his own name on the list and, if he could have afforded it, would have been open to any kind of therapy, just for himself. But he couldn't afford to pay and any psychotherapy offered on the National Health Service would have meant time off work, which again, he felt, was out of the question. The marriage broke up explosively before he ever got his marriage guidance appointment.

Bryan, the graphic designer, who admits to great bitterness towards his wife Cleo and an accompanying lack of objectivity, felt that she didn't give marriage guidance a fair try. He persuaded her to attend but only after she had told him she wanted the marriage to end. 'She was not a person to work at anything,' he said. 'So we only had a couple of attempts at counselling. If, according to the counsellors, my behaviour was deemed in any way to be in need of modification, she agreed. But when suggestions were made about how she could usefully change hers, that was all non-sense, of course.' So they carried on locked in battle on their own.

Architect Jeff admitted that he was responsible for the failure of Kay and himself to continue with marriage counselling. They made an agree-ment to go after they had separated but, by that time, they were embroiled in legal arguments over his access to the children. 'I was so angry and resentful about my few rights where the children were concerned and so bitter towards Kay that I didn't see any point in continuing to go to therapy.' He didn't at the time see that the sessions might have helped to dissipate some of the acrimony which was propelling them into exclusive, entrenched positions. He only knew that if she wasn't going to co-operate, neither was he. Since then, however, he has had personal therapy which, he says, did help him considerably to come to terms with himself and his situation.

Stuart very much wanted to go to marriage guidance with Celia after she had told him she wanted to end the marriage and was moving out for a while to give them both space to think. He went several times on his own and then once with Celia. 'But it is all about communication, isn't it, and as we had never discussed things in our marriage, by the time we got to guidance it was too late,' he said. The session was an eye-opener to him, however. 'The counsellor said he felt that Celia was no longer in love with me and didn't want to live with me, but she did need a lot of loving, which I wasn't giving.

'I can certainly see now that I wasn't loving for the last year of our marriage but I didn't see the break-up coming then.' It was Stuart who had said that he found it hard to be physically affectionate and that that had never been acknowledged or confronted in his marriage to Celia, despite whatever insecurity it may have caused her.

Quite a few men found therapy, whether their own or marriage guid-ance, helpful to them personally even if it didn't save the marriage. Jay, the deputy headmaster who had suppressed all his feelings about his first stillborn child, saw a psychiatrist because he had reached a state of clinical depression during the break-up of his marriage. It was then that he expressed himself for the first time and cried for the first time, a 'weakness' he had felt he wasn't allowed. But he still had a long way to go, in later failed relationships, before he could acknowledge and feel fully his own rights to all his own feelings.

It was many years after the stormy break-up of Pete's marriage to the flirtatious Pam that he became involved with encounter-type group therapy, through someone he had met at work. It was a lucky event for him as his background and lifestyle were such that he had never been exposed or open to the '60's surge towards personal growth, which perco-lated here from America.

'It affected me deeply,' he said, although initially he was extremely resistant and nervous. 'I now feel less of a sense of wrongness about what I do and have done. It makes me appreciate people's stroking of me. I don't feel I'm not worth it anymore.

'I also think much more about things. I was one of the big majority who didn't give a shit about what was going on in the world. I felt fuck all, and it was a selfish insular thing.'

It was the therapy, he feels, which made him come to terms with the decision he eventually came to about his children, one which has caused him considerable grief, and showed him how far he protected himself against caring for, and being cared for by other people after the hurt of his separation from Pam.

'I express my caring for people more and don't feel awkward about expressing it – I suppose I always felt it but suppressed it. I remember saying to a woman once that most people thought I was a very cold person and she said (I hardly knew her), "Oh no. I think you seem a lovely warm person." I found that very hard to believe but it really stuck in my mind, all the same.'

Book editor Frank and his wife Sarah did decide they had to do something to save their slowly deteriorating marriage when they had reached the point when sex had stopped and arguments were incessant. 'We talked about trying to do something but we didn't know what. Neither of us thought of sex therapy or anything like that. We didn't even know what marriage guidance was about.'

It so happened, however, that Frank was told about est at that time. est, always spelt in lower case, stands for Erhard Seminars Training, and is named after its founder Werner Erhard. It is a group technique that aims to help people see and change their lives and can very often seem extremely aggressive and confronting, especially to people who habitually repress strong emotions. Frank opted for est, despite his nervousness and reservations, because it seemed 'a possibility to jolt us'. Sarah, however, shied away.

'est was a turning point for me,' said Frank. 'I became very sure I wanted to make our marriage work whereas till then I would have ended it if she suggested it. est was a very emotional event for me, I cracked up in all directions.

'I had become worried that perhaps I was a homosexual, because I had ceased to want any sex with Sarah. But est showed me that I was just avoiding sex – as was my wife – because of our problems. Afterwards, I knew we had to talk about it, but she wouldn't discuss est and what had happened to me because she didn't approve of it.

'We did start going to marriage guidance separately, although we never got as far as the joint ones because she stopped. She felt it must be a waste of time because all she did at her sessions was cry. I imagine, though, that that was what she needed to do, because she didn't cry with me.

'A bit later, we did go to a weekend which was all about learning to communicate in marriage, and learning your own behaviour patterns in relationships. It was an extremely emotional experience for both of us. There was a great deal of emphasis on expressing feelings, however negative they seemed.

'It still makes me feel emotional to remember it. And I do think it was very effective. But, after it was over, we didn't really keep up what they had shown us, or the exercises they had recommended, like writing things down or setting time to talk. She said she was too busy with the children or I said I was working too hard. The pattern was that each of us would back off each time, each with different reasons. Perhaps neither of us by then really wanted to go on, so we didn't push the thing over the edge,' Frank reflected.

However, since the break-up of his marriage, he has personally carried on psychotherapy and also studied psychology, in an effort to understand more about human motivation and actions. He feels very strongly that the lack of any formal training or education in human behaviour is what damages so many relationships.

Inevitably, in a book on divorced men, counselling or therapy didn't 'work' as far as salvaging marriages is concerned, although that is not the inevitable aim of counselling in the first place. Often a couple may come to see that separation is their best course but may be helped to separate less acrimoniously or to learn quicker from past mistakes. Those who did not consider counselling often spent at least a few tortured years analysing themselves and their failures alone.

Of those who did get outside professional help, during or after their marriage break-up, some found the experience profound and feel they have a new and vital self-knowledge which may make all the difference as regards another successful relationship later.

Neal, witty, out-going, optimistic, feels he is a very different person from the screwed-up individual who went for a couple of marriage guidance sessions with his wife in the month before they parted.

'I told the counsellor that I was going to leave and he said fine. I was so shocked that it could be so easy that I stopped and thought again. The next time he attacked me for some of my feelings – my feeling that my wife was ugly, for instance (his wife was then recovering from anorexia) and my wish to leave the marriage, suggesting that I didn't trust women in general because of my relationship with my mother. She had been very ineffectual, as I saw it, but she also used to make threats when we were very young like taking us to borstal if we had been naughty and I hadn't realised how threatened and distrustful I had felt.

'I thought, as a result, that I must examine my attitudes to women and I went to see a psychotherapist at a hospital. But, due to an administrative bungle, I never got my follow-up appointments and didn't pursue them, so spent the several ensuing years grappling with my problems on my own.

'When you divorce, you tend to start meeting other divorced people, or, rather, the subject may get discussed more readily once you are in the same boat. I talked to a lot, their problems, their solutions and it was very helpful. One of them eventually put me in touch with a counselling service where I had weekly sessions for a couple of years.

'It was then that I realised that *I* had the right to feel sadness or anger or pain. It took all that time for me to grow up and get rid of my beliefs about duty and sacrifice. I was brought up to be told and to do and accept, and put myself second. But I now learned that you can't be loved unless you love yourself a bit. I had to learn I was a normal human being because I had become very selfish. Effectively I used to be self-sacrificing because it allowed me to ask favours.

'Because of my suppressed anger and distrust of women, all my relationships after my divorce lacked something, as far as I was concerned. The women weren't witty or interesting or beautiful enough – it was always *their* failure. And yet they were all devoted to me, because I clearly must have been the little boy lost. I know now that they were all marvellous people. But from where I was, I felt that women always held back from me while I was the most generous man in existence. I would entice them to love me and then run a mile. I had, subconsiously, to get my own back on women and I was capable of being very cruel.

'That has all gone now. And, over the last year, I have gradually got closer and closer to someone and we will probably decide to live together.'

Scriptwriter Morris, now fifty, is highly hang-dog about what he sees as more than a quarter of a century spent in emotional self-absorption. He had lost a marriage and one or two later long-term lovers before coming to psychotherapy. He was in the process of losing a third.

'Jean is a very wise woman. She could see I had problems. But as I continued to be unable to accept her as she was, she was backing off to protect herself and I was feeling panicky. A faint glimmer started to occur to me for the very first time in all my relationships that perhaps there was a tiny chance that I just *might* be in the wrong. Jean handed me some simple psychology books at just the right time.

'They became for me the most ghastly mirror, showing up all my manipulations and game-playing. So I went to a shrink to see if I could mend my ways and save myself losing Jean. I am making progress. I see myself as a shapeless sea creature, heaving and gasping at each stage of evolution. It can make me crumple with embarrassment to see the truth of my past behaviour, my selfishness and self-righteousness and brilliance at pushing guilt buttons – but it also makes me feel good.

'Jean and I have started getting on very well again. I have started accepting things which previously would have thrown me into terror. Like she can be friends with men she has known for years without that meaning she can't still love me. (I, of course, remained friends with numerous women I had known for years but that was entirely different!)

'If I had discovered so much earlier what I was really like, I would have saved so many lovely women so much pain.'

Marcus, who had rejected Rosalie's suggestion of going to marriage guidance on the grounds that they should be able to sort out their problems themselves, went to marriage guidance alone when Rosalie said she wanted a separation. 'I would have done anything then,' he remembered. 'But Rosalie wouldn't come with me. She seemed very determined and collected about her decision. But probably she was just being realistic, after all the soul-searching she at least had done already.

'I think I really did need that bombshell of her asking me to leave to wake me up, unfortunately. I was caught in a crisis the proportions of which I had no idea. When the crunch came, the floodgates finally opened. After my upbringing, I should have found marriage guidance difficult and resisted talking about my feelings, but by then I felt I had nothing to lose any more and I seemed to be able to talk and talk about everything.

'It has been *the* most significant experience of my life. I talked endlessly with Rosalie about what we should have done, where we went wrong. It was as if everything I had felt about what had happened to me in my life had been building up behind a wall and suddenly the wall had collapsed.

'It was like a revelation, definitely mystical. All sorts of things became crystal clear – my inability to face things, my fear of failure, everything – and I had this awful sense of "Oh, if only it could have happened before".

'Looking back, it would have needed an enormous amount of help and advice early on for us to have got over things – my repression of emotion, her insecurity and need for a father figure – but although the dice were loaded against us, we did have the makings of a terrific relationship. We just needed all the possible help we could have had.

'My marriage break-up, however tragic, has in fact for me been an opportunity for self-development. I was so desperate to believe it could be repaired that I would have faced anything, which is the only reason I got to marriage guidance. I have discovered and learned so much that makes sense of my experience of life. It has purpose and a pattern and it all fits together and I feel more in charge of it now.

'I would advise people to seek as much help as they need, to work on a marriage or work on how to part – whether they have children or not. A break-up can make you so much more entrenched in your mistrusts otherwise.'

# ═6═
# Divorce

Philosophical Malcolm, the printer, gives away nothing to belie his stated belief that marriage difficulties followed by divorce are just natural events in the history of relationships. Now, twelve years on, he shrugs and says: 'I was the one who pushed for the actual divorce but I think we both felt, "let's see if we can do any better". I mean, it isn't irrevocable, is it? In five years time, you could have another try if you wanted to.'

To most people, however, divorce marks a very definite end to marriage, so much so that some are reluctant to make it legal, even if there is no sign or hope of reconciliation. It was Ruth who turned down Dick's frenzied pleas to try again, after he had belatedly accepted he was a father and wanted his family, but it was also Ruth who pushed away the idea of divorce, reluctant to face fully that a second marriage had failed for her.

Scriptwriter Morris could not persuade his wife Alice to accept divorce, even though it was a secret longstanding affair of hers which had led to the break-up of their marriage, and she had since moved in with the boyfriend. 'She was neurotic even about a legal separation. I think she was hedging her bets,' he said. He had himself become involved with another woman and, as he put it, 'There had been a possibility of my marrying her but I couldn't get my divorce.

'People thought I was secretly colluding with my wife, thinking I might go back to her. It wasn't true. But she did often talk to me on the phone about our son or other things in a weirdly affectionate and wifely way. I found that creepy and definitely wanted a divorce.'

But, as he will admit, remaining legally married also served an unwitting purpose for him because he in fact was reluctant to commit himself to his new lover and the relationship didn't last, after his eventual divorce. Neal made a similar use of his elongated married status, though at the time he saw it as a generous period of inaction undergone on his wife's behalf. 'I told her that I wouldn't be marrying again, so divorce didn't bother me but that if she wanted one, that was fine, as long as it didn't involve me in time or expense.

'It was four years later that she started a postal divorce. Till then, I suppose I had felt sort of protected against other women because I was still married. Certainly a couple whom I had become quite strongly involved with felt insulted because I wasn't even bothering with divorce.'

Changes in divorce laws over the past fifteen years have helped couples where one partner is intransigent about divorce (five years' separation is sufficient grounds without the partner's consent) and, more recently, have also put the emphasis on reducing the acrimony that can occur over grounds, property and children. As much as possible is done to help couples agree among themselves the arrangements they wish to come to, rather than rely on and resent the imposition of a court's conclusions. Conciliation services have been set up to help.

Other changes in the law mean that wives are no longer automatically entitled to what men call a 'meal ticket' for life, i.e. maintenance for themselves as well as the children. The introduction of divorce after two years' separation with consent also did away with the need to lay 'blame' or guilt on one partner by proving adultery, desertion or unreasonable behaviour.

However much the changes were thought by many to act against women's interests, not so much has really changed at all in that respect. Far from fears that wives would be dumped when they ceased to seem exciting to capricious males, it is women who file more divorces than men. And although judges are not obliged to require a husband to pay a wife maintenance, they are only likely not to do so where the marriage has been short and there are no children. Many couples also opt not to wait for the emotionally easier separation for two years with consent. For the sake of speed, one party still divorces the other (usually the man) on the grounds of adultery, desertion or unreasonable behaviour – the last often requiring such a long list of trivial (or untrue) accusations that the end result is unlikely to be amicable.

So divorce still leaves many men, at least, feeling that their interests and rights, to say nothing of their images, are less kindly looked upon in courts. The main bones of contention are over property, money, custody and access, though not necessarily all or any, I found.

Only Bryan, still bitter over the break-up of his marriage, felt passionately that the scales of justice had tipped too far in Cleo's favour in all respects.

'My wife worked on a woman's magazine before we married and could easily have carried on as a freelance journalist if she had wanted to later, but she didn't. Now the children are fourteen and ten and she is only thirty-eight, but she won't consider working. She sits at home painting her toenails while I send on the cheque.

'I sold our house and some other assets and bought her another house for cash, while I now live in a flat with a very large mortgage. I have to pay her not to work, as well as paying for the children and for their private education.

'We had agreed that I would have the children every other weekend and Thursday evening of the week I didn't see them. But once she had got everything she wanted out of the settlement, she started saying it was too disruptive for the children if I saw them in the week as well. She wants to take them on a trip to America to see her cousin and is now saying that if I agree to finance that, she'll let me see them fortnightly midweek. I am having to buy my children! And I didn't even want the marriage to break up.

'I feel I have got nothing, and I'm not even independent anymore. I'm a freelance graphic designer but I can't take the risk of being out of work with all these bills, so I have had to take a part-time job, just to be certain of some regular income. It may mean having to turn down bigger jobs when they come, because I haven't the capacity to take them on, though I'm having to work all hours as it is.

'I don't believe a man should have to pay for his wife, in circumstances like mine, where she could work. Nor do I think I should be the only one of us who has to pay for the children. I know now why some men disappear. If it weren't for my vast love of my children, I'd do a bunk myself.'

Many men who gladly paid all they could for their children were still appalled to find themselves and their partners wrangling over property and money.

Marcus, the American studies teacher who developed writer's block, agreed with Rosalie that she should have the house, and the children would live with her, although custody would be joint. That meant they would share decisions about the children's futures.

'I had acted irresponsibly till then, I felt, and so joint custody was important to me, to make me feel responsible, and *capable* of that kind of responsibility at last. Emotionally I felt more responsible for our break-up, even though there were factors on both sides.

'I therefore felt nervous on the children's part, however, that if I signed over the whole house to Rosalie, my children would be at the mercy of a stepfather who would inherit should she marry again but die before him. I wanted to retain a part in trust for the children but Rosalie saw that as undermining her security. She admits she needed to feel she was right to leave me and that, if we split everything equally, it was as if she were equally to blame.

'We tried all ways round it. She suggested that if I kept a forty per cent interest in the house, I should pay forty per cent of the mortgage. It sounded reasonable to me, but my solicitor said no, because I would never personally have an interest in the house. It did get acrimonious. I found I couldn't talk to her directly about the mortgage because we just brought up everything else as well and then I would crumple with guilt. So it was all done through solicitors in the end. We agreed on the house being in her name and the children only having an interest in it after her death.'

Dan, whose marriage had ended when he started an affair, wanted to do the best by his wife and son. 'I said to the solicitor, let's split it all half and half. He said, "If you do that, she'll want more." "She is not that kind of person," I told him, but he said. "She will be. And even if she isn't, her solicitor is."

'My wife had always been a competent secretary but she went to court and said she couldn't work because of the child. She got herself five eighths of my salary and then went out and got a job as well.'

Joe, whose wife became estranged from him after a stillbirth, feels strong resentment about property division, not as far as his first wife was concerned but his second. His first wife left him for another man and he was the one who looked after the children.

'She filed for a divorce straightaway but she never claimed a part of the home then or any maintenance for herself. When I married again and sold the house, she let us take two thirds and took only one third herself. But when my second marriage broke up, I had to give the second one half the house and I feel it was really unfair, because of all the grafting I had done to get the money for it in the first place.

'I resented it because she hadn't contributed anything to the house and it was a lot of money. My first wife *had* grafted with me and she, I feel, was certainly entitled to half, although she didn't want it. I suppose it was because she had walked out on me and left the children with me too. But the second one came in on the tail end of things and reaped it.

'A friend of mine has his girlfriend living with him in his house but he won't let her pay for anything, in case they split up and then she won't have grounds to claim. That can't help a relationship much, can it? But I can well understand. My kids are all grown up now and I own a really nice house. I don't want someone coming in and claiming half of that too.'

Bill, a painter and decorator who had been married for 12 years, is still bemused about why his marriage broke up. He adored his wife and remembers with a bitter nostalgia the Christmas card she sent him the year before, saying she loved him more than ever. He felt so fiercely that the marriage could be pieced together again, despite her affair with another man, that he started by contesting the divorce. 'But the solicitor advised me against going on with it because it would be very expensive and she would *still* get her divorce.'

There was no wrangling between them over the children, as it was quite clearly believed by them both that the children should see each of them as and when they wanted. But what Bill saw as Louise's grasping attitude to money hurt him very much. He says he would have given her anything she wanted but she took without asking or even saying, perhaps out of a fear that bitterness would affect Bill's behaviour.

He had been badly hurt, for instance, to receive her petition on grounds of unreasonable behaviour. 'It was the only grounds she could come up with. I showed it to the children and they agreed it was a pack of lies. I was supposed to have abused her verbally, criticised her dress and commented on her make-up (she never wore any before she met that bloke).'

Eventually he gave in and allowed the divorce on those grounds. Louise sought and was granted temporary custody but, when it became clear that three of the children, the sons, wanted to be with their father, she and Bill agreed that he would have custody and stay in the house with them, while she was rehoused by the council, with their daughter.

'When she left, she virtually gutted the place. I think she was frightened. She had thought she would have the house and kids, and now it seemed she had nothing. She took all the furniture, the sheets, the crockery and cutlery, all the ornaments – anything she thought was worth anything, even things that had been personal gifts to me.

'When I had moved out, before we decided I would have the children, I was paying towards the mortgage and maintenance for her and the children, and I carried on, even though I had them later and she was the one claiming the family allowance. She still ran up debts on the mortgage, which I am left with. Now she wants her share of the house, which she is legally entitled to. But I can't re-mortgage, to pay her off, and I really don't want to have to move into a flat. The children have always had a garden and freedom. Why should they have to suffer because of our broken marriage?

'I still give Louise anything I can. She got money from the council for a cooker, but I bought one for her, so she could use that money for something else. It was how she acted that has hurt. She moved everything out of our house and stored it at her parents' on a day I was out with the children. I didn't even know it was happening.'

For him, the worst part of divorcing was being obliged to live together but separately while the divorce came through. 'It was agony. She brought a brick wall down. She wouldn't have anything I had cooked, or cook for me. That was a lot to do with what solicitors tell you – you mustn't be seen to be living together in any real sense. But if one person wants the marriage back, it is excruciatingly painful to go through.'

Solicitors were singled out as the creators rather than the solvers of problems by many men. Malcolm who sounded so philosophical about divorce felt less so about solicitors. 'They were an evil bunch of jackals,' he said. 'They refused to agree whereas my wife and I had never argued. They figure that, if you make a deal with your wife, they haven't got a job – or a nice big bill coming. So they try to poison you against each other.

'They said she should be going for more. We had agreed that I buy her a house and keep her and the kids. But the lawyers wanted a different deal. They wanted me to sell our house, give her a lump repayment and then let her rent! It was ridiculous. We stuck out and won. As it is, she had a lovely house which she sold for plenty later and now she and her new husband have an even better one.

'She was confused at the time by what the lawyers were saying and thought she might be losing out if she did it our way. But it was the complete reverse. I took out another mortgage to buy her house. I didn't resent any of it. You've got to stand by your responsibilities, and it didn't really affect me. So I couldn't afford a nice car, so what?'

One couple who didn't have children decided to 'do our own divorce, using the book. But dividing money was a big problem because no one has set down the facts and figures of the "norm" in settlements,' said the man. 'I think it is a conspiracy by lawyers that this can't be done. As it was, of course, we found *our* expectation of the norm totally different from each other's.

'She felt she ought to be maintained, even though she was working. I didn't, although I ended up maintaining her for a few years. I agreed in the end to figures I felt were reasonable, plus some for goodwill, but she resented having to fight for it all, even though she was happy enough with the outcome.'

Anxiety over arrangements about children was less than over property in most cases, most usually because both partners wanted to do best by their children's needs, however much they wrangled over their own. In some cases however, the wife felt the husband's access claims were unreasonably high, such as every other weekend, plus one week night every fortnight, whereas the husband felt that was not a lot to compensate for not living with their children any more. Sometimes the wrangling over children set the scene for more longstanding bitterness and resentment.

As one said: 'The seeds of resentment do seep in. I now resent the fact that I will be paying out for my wife for a long time yet, because she hasn't got a proper job and isn't likely to try to get one. I feel I've been generous, yet she takes my money for granted. I find myself criticising her as a mother – sometimes on her weekends with the children, she isn't even there much of the time and leaves them with her sister. But I try to keep my mouth shut. I didn't want a big drawn out fight at the time, and so I didn't push.

'I'll avoid seeing her when I collect the children, if I can. And whereas I used to try to be helpful if she needed to change an arrangement, now I'll only do it if it suits me.'

Another felt very isolated as a father, not because the courts had not granted him fair access but because his wife and her family tried to freeze him out. 'She refused to accept the maintenance she was granted for herself and our child because she and her parents felt that it strengthened my rights if I was paying and effectively they didn't want me to have any. She even tried to get me to relinquish all hold of the child so that her new boyfriend, whom she was to marry, could adopt him. It sounded dreadfully final to me and I felt very confused about what was best for the boy. In the end I refused, despite the fact that they made it very difficult for me to see him.'

Architect Jeff and his wife Kay, who had parted by mutual consent after several trial separations, had come to no formal decision about access, as Jeff hadn't wished to be tied down. However, by the time the divorce was going through, he had met another woman. 'I think Kay was very jealous. She started going through massive mood swings and sometimes she would be pleasant and co-operative about the children, other times manipulative and obstructive. I became very wary and slightly worried that access had been left to us to sort out, rather than set by the court. At times I didn't get to see the children because she said they didn't like my girlfriend and didn't want to come. Maybe that was true. Or was she manipulating them?

'You don't know what to do for the best, in the end.'

Men who wanted custody of their children usually didn't find it easy to get. When Robert called a halt to his marriage after he caught his wife with a man for a second time, they had a court battle for custody of Mandy. 'I think one of the reasons I won,' he said, 'was that my wife had nowhere stable to live. She had left our home and was living with one man after another. At court, I had to stand up and give my reasons for why I should have custody and that meant giving all the details of what had happened, how I found her with those men. It was so humiliating. I wanted the ground to swallow me. In the end, the judge said, "No one could make up a story like that," and I won.

'I was only ordered to pay her maintenance of 5p – a token amount, the lowest you could then have – but I decided not to be mean and gave her £5 a week. But I had Mandy made a ward of court because I was terrified she would be snatched while I was at work. As a ward of court, neither of us could take her out of the country without express court permission.'

Nick, unemployed, feels he only has custody of his daughter because of an administrative bungle. He was granted temporary custody when his wife left him with the child but the case to decide permanent custody didn't come up when it should have. Although his ex-wife now wants custody, and the case is pending, he feels he shouldn't lose his daughter, having cared for her for two years.

By no means all the divorces involved acrimony as regards the settlement of money and parental affairs, even when a lot of emotional misery and anger had been expressed beforehand.

Italian Tony is happy that, despite what he looks back on as his self-indulgent, hysterical behaviour while divorce was being discussed, the arrangements made in the end were agreed calmly. 'The divorce only took five minutes because we had agreed amicably before about what I should pay and that my access to the children should be open.'

Men who had felt they were responsible for the marriage collapse were particularly willing and eager to be generous, however disenchanted they might have been feeling towards their wives. Charles had felt Deborah was also to blame for the failure of their marriage, although it was his affair with Maria that initiated the actual ending.

'I bought her a house and paid for both her and the children, even though she was working. She earned nowhere near as much as I did and I certainly didn't want her in hardship. It was the least I could do. I felt I *should* pay her. I felt a very strong sense of duty towards her because I did feel I had done her injury in some ways.' He did insist on joint custody, however, despite Deborah's initial resistance, because he wanted to retain his responsibility for his children. Without joint custody, a father has no legal right to shared decisions over education or anything important to the well-being of the child.

Dave, who had walked out very suddenly on his wife Anthea and the children, gladly gave all he could to his wife when he realised how much he was hurting them all merely by his nominal presence. 'I gave her the house, the contents, the bank balance, the car, everything. I had just my suitcase.'

Guilt made Jay make a decision he might have regretted when he divorced Shelley and became clinically depressed. He, too, gladly gave over the house and paid her and for Vicky, his daughter. 'And because we remained friends, access was free. But Shelley did get me to sign an agreement that she could take Vicky out of the country. Shelley was Canadian-born and her parents still lived there. I knew she wanted to go back and, because I felt so guilty, I gave her the licence to go. I don't think I understood then what it would be like with Vicky so far away, but when it came to it there was nothing I could do about it anyway, of course.'

Couples without children inevitably had it easier as regards the mechanics of divorce but didn't necessarily escape all problems. As one man explained: 'Although we had agreed on a split up of things and money, once the divorce came along all the niggling started – over piddling amounts. The financial wrangling was symbolic rather than anything else but it meant that the divorce was an emotionally tiring experience when it needn't have been at all.'

In so far as divorce does symbolise the failure to have made an important loving relationship work, its emotional impact is by no means negligible for childless couples. Ben made a point of going through his very gently with Gail, who at first was reluctant to agree to one. They were the two who had had their own sets of parents divorce acrimoniously and both had been fearful of any such repeat on their own parts.

'Gail didn't think the separation would last. She claimed she still loved me, despite breaking our vow to be faithful to each other, and was very upset and insecure. We took it slowly. I moved out but paid my share of the rent on our flat. I didn't press for divorce but said we needed a legal separation to clarify our tax positions.

'We would let large patches of time go by and then meet and settle some small aspect. It wasn't upsetting or fraught, although there was a sense of dissociation. My mother said: "What about the jewellery I gave her?" I said: "You gave it to her. It is hers. I'm not getting it back."

'Neither of us tried to get things out of each other. We felt it was all very equitable in the end. We made an inventory of things which were uncontentious and then divided mutual things later. In fact, we just picked one each, in turn, until we reached the end of the list. It felt very painless that way and we felt good about it.

'The actual divorce was done by post.' He smiled wryly. 'We didn't manage the divorce party we had always promised ourselves, should we decide to part. But we did achieve an amicable divorce and we both feel relieved and more respectful of each other because of it.'

Coming out of divorce with self-respect was seen as very important in retrospect by many, even those who felt that things had not turned out as they had wished.

'Try to do your utmost so that the kids won't suffer,' said one. 'Be honest with them. Parents should be shot for having a tug-of-war over children.'

And another: 'If the wife wants to go, the best thing a man can do, if he loves the child and once loved the lady, is make it as easy for her as he can. Showing generosity may make her re-think. But even if it doesn't, you at least have continued to do your best for your child and your wife.'

# —7—
# Children-
# living apart

'I feel something irreplaceable has been taken away from me. I am being deprived of years of fatherhood, which is not like a death but like a long serious illness,' said graphic designer Bryan, with heartfelt pain when talking about his children whom he now sees every other weekend. 'Even if, at 16, they suddenly decided that they wanted to live with me, I can't put back those four or eight lost years.'

Losing real contact with children, ceasing to be able to act and influence as a full-time father and fear of being replaced in their lives worries most fathers living apart, especially those who have an access to their children that isn't as open as they would like. They naturally fear the consequences of the marriage break-up on a child's emotional development, guilt compounding loss. Men I spoke to made the troubled transition from full-time to weekend father with differing amounts of dis-ease, depending on their circumstances, arrangements and relationships with their ex-wives.

Bryan, two years' divorced, still feels a keen sense of unreality about his present style of parenting and, because he did not want his marriage to end, feels not guilt but blame against his former wife which, as he admits, is not constructive.

'When you have been married with children for ten years or more, life becomes so unreal alone. I have no difficulty cooking for the children, or looking after them, and I give them a lot when I see them but then it is nothing, silence, for two weeks.

'I feel they get manipulated by both of us. I also feel at an extra disadvantage because, as I am having to work so hard to pay everything I have to pay to Cleo, that cuts into the time I have with my children. Often when they are here, I am having to work. I feel bitter that Cleo, because she can live so comfortably, and doesn't have to work, can create a relaxed, easy-going atmosphere in her house, whereas in mine it is all rush and interruptions.

'I worry about the children's feelings but don't feel I should push them further than they want to go, in talking about them. I do very much regret giving in to Cleo and trying to keep the fact we were breaking up a secret. They obviously realised something was going on but didn't get a chance to talk. When my twelve-year-old son said he hoped I wouldn't be lonely, I took it as a chance to ask how he was taking our being apart. "Oh fine," he said, "I'm over it" but of course he isn't. Still, it meant that the subject was opened and we could come back to it sometimes, when it felt right.

'I remember my daughter said nothing about what had happened for months. Then one day we were round at the house of a little friend of hers who said that her parent's were taking her to a pantomime. And my daughter suddenly said to all of us, "I used to be taken to things with both my mummy and daddy before they separated." I wanted to burst out crying.

'Research says that children would rather have two parents together, even if they argue, and I'm terribly aware of that.

'A priceless thing is gone. And all it takes is for someone to say, "I don't love you anymore." '

Marcus, the American studies teacher whose repressed emotions finally flooded out during counselling, is grateful that he and Rosalie have remained able to cooperate and communicate over the children. Four years have passed but he recalls: 'It was easy to relate to them because they were so young. But they would say, "When are you coming back?" 'I wish you could live with us", and imagining the anguish they must be feeling was very painful, especially as I was so desperate to patch things up with Rosalie anyway.

'We agreed that I could come every weekend to see them, on a Saturday. Sometimes now they spend the weekend with me, or I there, if Rosalie is away. It has paid off, remaining in good contact with Rosalie, because we are able with little difficulty, to be with the children together on special occasions, like Christmas.

'I don't feel difficulty handing the children back after they have been with me but I know that, inside, I deeply resent feeling that I have been cheated of my children by some obscure and malignant god. I don't see a way of getting over that. I feel cheated even of the daily routine and chores of children. There is something a bit unreal about seeing them just for a day, and I feel that they must see *me* as unreal. I do feel lonely but I often feel that most when I am with the children – aware that it is just us and not mother and father and the children.

'Rosalie now has a boyfriend who lives with her. I was very jealous and hurt by that initially and I didn't want him acting as father to my children. However, he is also divorced and has children who don't live with him. So he is very sympathetic in that aspect, which comforted me a lot and allayed my resentment.

'My big problem now is that I do feel insecure about providing somewhere for the children to be when they get older. I pay rent in a shared house and I doubt, in the prevailing economy, that I will be able to afford to buy a flat of my own. I am not security conscious for myself but I know I will need two bedrooms and a living room for the children. One is a girl and the boys are unlikely to want to sleep with me when they get older. I feel very daunted about what is going to happen on that score.'

None of the men I spoke to expressed serious worries about coping with the practicalities of child-care on their own, partly because many happened to have participated in the practicalities during their marriages or because, when the divorce happened, the children were old enough for that not to be a problem. Certainly some remember not cooking at all; they all ate out, and the children saw that as a treat. Of more common concern was how to behave with their children.

Jeff, the architect, said: 'I was always adept at caring for the children – cooking, nappies, entertaining them, things like that. But I found that when I had them for the weekend on my own, I could become angry and irritated with them. I wanted to know whether that happened to other divorced fathers, because it made me feel guilty. Cooking, making beds, reading to them, giving them constant attention – I found it a strain. I felt it was different for mothers, they have them all the time, it's just normal life. Whereas for the father, the children are just on a visit and you feel that everything should be lovely all the time.

'I also had difficulty knowing how much time to spend with them. At first I tried to do things with them all the time, plan special things for just us and not include their friends. But it was too much in the end, so now we don't plan whole weekends anymore.

'We have established a pattern now. At the beginning, it was dreadful. When I took them back to their house, they would hang on to me, not let me go. We all cried. I wanted them every weekend but Kay wouldn't agree. Now I see them one night in the week and every other weekend and that suits me too. I couldn't handle them every weekend. I need some social life of my own.

'I know the children adore me and I think now that they are less affected by the separation than I am. You can't keep phoning and they don't phone you between times. My sadness is that they haven't known a normal family life. It is so unnatural when we are together – like that empty car seat where mum used to sit. But they take it very much for granted, it seems. They don't seem to recognise the difference, perhaps because they haven't know any different for so long. Maybe, in their case, the effects won't be so profound as I always fear.

'The irony is that I spend more time with them now than if I were married – really with them, that is. I do feel a little fearful of feeling left out, if Kay married someone else and he was a good man and became part of the family unit. But I wouldn't feel jealous over Kay. I also worry about how my children would feel if I married again and had another child.

'I'm resigned now, though, to having less influence over my children's lives than I could have had.'

Joe, the lab technician whose wife started an affair during her depression over a stillbirth, looked after his children for some years before they went back to their mother. He can identify with Jeff's feelings of uncertainty over how to behave for the best.

'I had them on Sundays and, sure, if they were naughty and I told them off, I felt guilty. They feel so precious because they are all you've got and so it hurts to tick them off. It's a tug of war. But you can't let them get away with things, otherwise they get spoilt, even though you don't want to upset them because you see them so rarely. And though you fear you are going to lose their love, of course you don't.

'I never resented the fact that they were living with their mother and another man. I knew the kids always felt *I* was their dad.' Two of Joe's children, those of his first marriage, are grown up now and he has an extremely close relationship with both of them.

Frank found his relationship with his children much more natural during times of separation pre-divorce than it was after the separation became final. He used to see them frequently, because he babysat on evenings when Sarah wanted to go out and had them at the house if she went away for the weekend. He had been used to looking after children, so the responsibility wasn't daunting. But that kind of cooperation ceased after he moved out permanently to a bedsit he found through an advertisement in the paper.

'I started seeing the children every fortnight. I took them out for the day, which was very difficult. What do you do in a small town on a Sunday when everything is closed? I had moved to London and wanted to bring them to stay with me, but Sarah wouldn't agree for some time. By then I had got a better place to live.

'I remember that things I normally wouldn't care about I had to care about, otherwise Sarah would take it out on me and make things difficult. The little boy liked to climb things, for instance, and would ruin his clothes. I'd get a bollocking when I took him back like that, so I started making demands about his behaviour and getting irritable if he scuffed his shoes. I ended up feeling resentful towards my wife and guilty about my son, especially as my own father had been strict that way with me.

'But there was pleasure in the time we spent, both for me and the children. It only started getting really complicated when I met my current wife and suddenly the children were visiting both of us, not just me.'

The physical dilemma of where to take children, if visiting them entailed travelling to a different town, was mentioned by a few people. 'Every week you end up wandering round the museum.' For some men, however, the problems were of much greater geographical proportions. Dick, who only after he split up from Ruth seven years ago realised that he cared that he had a son at all, now sees his son only twice a year. Ruth has remarried and is temporarily living abroad because of her new husband's job. By the time they moved there, three years ago, Dick had established a strong relationship with his son Tim.

'I lived around the corner from Ruth, so I used to pop in a couple of evenings a week, to say goodnight to him, and saw him all day Sundays. We would walk down canals, go out in boats, play in the park. I normally have a low boredom threshold but, even though times weren't always exciting together, I never felt I wanted to see less of him.

'I found I had tremendous patience with him, not a feature I'm famous for. He did irritate me sometimes but I didn't show it. There were certainly times when I felt he would like to see more of me but I know that that wouldn't have happened, even if I had still been living with Ruth. He would usually be asleep when I got home and I'm dreadful in the mornings. I did find, though, that if he were ill, I would leave work early especially to come see him, which I wouldn't have done if I had still been with Ruth.'

So Tim had become a very important part of Dick's life by the time Ruth and her new husband Andrew told him of the four-year posting in Germany. Ruth by then also had another child.

'I accept the reason why they wanted to go,' said Dick. Andrew's job, when based in London, had meant that he was continually obliged to travel away for months at a time and there was no real family life. 'I accepted it and agreed, because Ruth had been unhappy and that was no good for Tim either, but I wasn't happy about it, of course.

'I would certainly like to be closer to Tim. I think about the things we could be doing together. I miss having some involvement in his learning, both formal and informal. I think there are a lot of things I could open his interest in, which Ruth or Andrew can't because they don't share those interests – in computers, for instance.'

He knows that he is welcome to stay in Germany as often as he likes and as long as he likes but denies that he could, if he wanted, spend more time there than he does. 'My work doesn't make it easy to get away a lot (he works for himself) but, okay, yes, I still do have my own life to lead, and I don't feel that comfortable in Germany.

'I certainly don't resent Andrew acting as Tim's father, though. I know he does his absolute best for Tim and cares about him a lot. Tim calls him Andrew but I am dad.'

Little Vicky, at two years old, was the centre of Jay's existence when his marriage collapsed. Although he had signed a form allowing Shelley to take her out of the country, and knew she might have it in mind to go to her parents in Canada, he put the possibility out of his own thoughts at first. He was in a very confused, still depressed state at the time.

'I had Vicky for five days every other weekend and that was enough to give me a very strong sense of continuity in her life. I had given Shelley the house but because the flat I then rented was close by, I would also often drop in during the week or babysit. Vicky got used to it. She was a child who had two households but plenty of warmth. Shelley and I never criticised each other around her. We were both sad rather than bitter that our marriage hadn't worked.

'So being separate from Vicky didn't really hit me until, two years later, Shelley decided to go back to Canada to live with her parents on their farm and finish the degree in modern languages that she had abandoned to come here. I don't remember the decision as a bombshell because it probably came together bit by bit. But I didn't have an inkling what it would be like. We agreed that Vicky would spend the summers with me, for three months, and for the next five years I just made sure I got over to Canada somehow or other, in my Christmas and Easter school holidays.

'Being with Vicky was the one thing I did well, the one thing I didn't need reassurance about. When I put her back on the plane after the summer, I was dysfunctional for at least two weeks.

'She used to want to know why she couldn't have both of her parents at the same time. Even the same country would have been enough! But the agony ended for me at least when, at ten years old, she decided she wanted to live here in England.'

Many fathers who did not have to cope with such a geographical distance felt there were very positive aspects to separate parenting, either because of their heightened awareness of their children as separate people or because of the good easy-going arrangements agreed with ex-partners.

Tony was one of the former. He had moved away to the next town after agreeing that Beth's new husband-to-be should move into their house with the children. The children came to stay with Tony at weekends. 'It was the first time I had been on my own with them but coping practically wasn't a problem at all. At weekends, ninety-nine per cent of the time we had a real ball. I gave them far more attention than I had when I lived with them.' Tony was one of the men who had had difficulty adapting to the restrictions of married life and had wanted to spend quite a lot of time on activities with friends that didn't necessarily involve the children. 'I used to be irritable at home with the children,' he said. 'But I wasn't anymore. It was different.I didn't feel I had the right to take them for granted. They were little individuals, not part of an ordinary family set-up anymore.

'I saw my role in life as a dual one. At weekends I was father with no mum and I enjoyed that. I enjoyed their company and finding out more about them. But, on Sunday night, when I dropped them off, I became a single man again.

'At first I did spend a lot of that time worrying about them. I wasn't fully relaxed with the situation for two years. My daughter went through a lot of heartache. She wasn't happy about Beth's new husband and there were quite a few behaviour problems. She would attack the husband and then, when she was criticised, felt picked on. There were dreadful emotional scenes initially when I arrived to collect them. She would fly out of the house and fling her arms round me.

'She said she wanted to live with me and, if I felt I could have managed, I would have taken her without hesitating. So I found all that emotionally disturbing. But when my daughter was eleven and started a new school, she made a lot of new friends, became very popular and considerably happier. She is stable now, I think.

'My son is now sixteen. He always got on well with his step-father. They both enjoy practical activities which they do together. He seems to have no hang-ups about my leaving, it was all very normal to him.

'Beth's husband said at the start that he wouldn't be a father to the children, he would be a friend. If anything, I regret that he wasn't really friends with them. I felt he saw them as my children and wasn't 100 per cent happy about taking them on. But things got better when he and Beth had a child of their own.

'I now see the children fortnightly, for practical reasons. I work Saturday mornings and I wanted to have some Saturday nights free. I don't think the children would appreciate being left! Also, there are activities at home that they are involved in at weekends. They want to have a chance to do things with their friends.

'My main regret is that my influence, as a father, is reduced by only seeing them every other weekend. If my daughter has a problem, she may talk to me on the telephone but you can guide children much more easily within a family situation. If something bothers one of them, there just isn't time to sort it all out in one weekend. My daughter tends to baulk at talking about her feelings, so I have to come on at an angle, so to speak.

'Looking at them now, I don't think they have suffered badly. There have definitely been benefits, such as more attention received from Beth and me separately – although obviously a happy marriage where that amount of attention is given is considerably better. I do expect my daughter to have some problems with her adult relationships, as a result of what went on. She hasn't really sorted out her own emotions about my leaving and another man physically taking my place.

'But she is a tough, strong kid. When I was there, she was shy and withdrawn.'

Lew's daughter, now sixteen, was eight when he and Judy split up. The marriage had died its death some years earlier but they had deliberately stayed together till they felt Grace was old enough to understand. Despite the fact that their life together had been largely depressing and unhappy, according to Lew, he and Judy stayed friends and cooperated fully over Grace.

'We told her what was happening and what it meant in terms of the pattern of her life. But in many ways, her life didn't change much at all,' he said. 'She only moved a couple of doors away, she still had the same friends, Judy and I still saw each other. I saw Grace almost daily – she popped round or stayed, or I went round to Judy's, even though Martin, her live-in lover, wasn't too comfortable about that.

'I was far too close by to be threatened by Martin taking over as a father. It never even occurred to me as a problem. I even feel that the experience of relating to both him and me might have been useful to Grace.'

Like Tony, however, he does expect her to have suffered psychologically, despite the fact that he doesn't feel the actual separation was tremendously traumatic for her.

'She is not overly confident and I expect that is partly to do with Judy and me parting. I'm working on that, but she is going to have to make her own life. Yes I do feel guilt that what we did has affected her, just as my parents' separation affected me. I used to feel guilt a lot but now that's much less because I accept that I can't change things. All I can do is take any opportunity that occurs to make something good. No doubt she will go through her angst in her twenties or thirties – but hopefully *before* she has children.'

Judy moved to another town when Grace was thirteen and Grace then came to stay with Lew at weekends.

'Then I did have some problems establishing a relationship where there was enough attention but without spoiling her,' he said. 'Because our meetings had become timetabled, she became more concerned about the amount of attention she received; and apparently I didn't give enough. She said she wanted more demonstrations of my affection – not necessarily physical. I would give her my complete attention for periods but not all the time because I didn't think that right to do. It couldn't have been all wrong because our relationship is an extremely good one.'

Dave knew that he was taking a large gamble on his children's feelings when he suddenly walked out on them and Anthea. They had heard, if not seen, the emotionally violent scene that ensued when he came straight into the house and upstairs to pack a suitcase to leave, and the youngest of the four had pursued him in tears to the gate. Dave told them all that he would be in touch very soon and made himself not turn his head, even as his youngest stood there calling his name.

'The children were terribly shaken,' he remembers, four years later. 'I saw the two boys within a couple of weeks. I had to meet them at the corner of the road because Anthea didn't want me in the house. I was told that the two girls didn't want to see me. They were sixteen and seventeen and could make up their own minds. The boys were twelve and fourteen.

'There was nowhere to go with the boys except the local Wimpy. I remember that their biggest concern was that *I* was okay. I was careful to say nothing against Anthea at all. I just told them that we were incompatible and it didn't mean that either of us loved them any the less.

'Anthea felt very bitter towards me but we did talk on the phone about the children. Then I saw my elder daughter in the street and she burst into tears and flung her arms round me. It was a wonderful feeling, knowing she hadn't rejected me after all. I started seeing them all, and also returned to the house, to sort possessions out.

'Anthea told me that all the children were acting oddly for them. The boys were truanting from school, the girls weren't doing their homework, they had all become trouble-makers. I talked to them. I said, "Look, you are old enough not to let what has happened affect *your* lives. It has happened and that is that." They did get better after that.

'I saw them once a week or fortnightly and they would phone me, although Anthea wouldn't let me phone them. I could only see them in the day, though, because I had nowhere to take them. I was sleeping on sofas. Because they were older, it was more like seeing friends than seeing children. We enjoyed our times together. But it was difficult if they had problems because I was in no position to sort them out on the spot.

'It has all worked out surprisingly well. I now see them once every few weeks or once a month, when they have space for *me*. They are busy leading their own lives now. They get on surprisingly well with my new wife and adore our little kid. They have all left school and have also left home and seem to enjoy their freedom,' he said. He is not dismissive of the emotional trauma he knows that he caused them, but relieved that they appear to have adjusted and accepted.

Charles' children were aged fourteen and seventeen when he confessed to Deborah his years' long affair with Maria and moved out, pending either reconciliation or divorce. He had managed his double life without thinking about the ramifications of its exposure, a deliberately blinkered approach, he admits, to avoid facing what he saw as his double bind situation – a dissatisfaction in his marriage and a horror of divorce, because his own parents' divorce had been so traumatic to him.

'I was terrified the children would turn against me and reject me,' he said. 'But they didn't *seem* upset, although I now know my daughter was deeply unhappy at the time. She had difficulties at school and saw a psychologist for some while. My son wasn't so affected. He said he felt it made him grow up very quickly. He also tended to look upon me as a protector and felt that he would have more of me to himself, if I wasn't with Deborah. I think they both sensed how very deeply attached I was to them.

'I was still haunted by what had happened with my parents and I had determined that I would never inflict on my children what they had inflicted on me. It seemed I had failed horribly but, in retrospect, I think I was successful after all in that. I really loved them and wanted the best for them. I saw them all the time, because the flat I bought was round the corner. I would pop round, take them out, collect them from school, take them on holidays abroad. They don't seem to have trouble forming rela-tionships with the opposite sex (they are all over eighteen now), they don't

seem emotionally disturbed. I don't think *my* parents were much interested in me or my sisters and that was what made the difference.

'My daughter even got reasonably close to Maria, though the boy
wasn't too interested in her.'

Droll and self-deprecating, Morris felt he had a very charmed relationship with his twelve-year-old son Paul, after he had moved into his
cold bedsitter. ('I used to complain to Alice that I couldn't afford better
because she was bleeding me dry, but that was just another attempt at guilt
buttons.') Alice had revealed to him that she wouldn't go ahead with their
proposed move to the country because she couldn't bear to leave the man
she had secretly been having an affair with for several years and that had
precipitated their parting.

'I lived close by and spent most evenings at the house with Paul, while
Alice was out trying to rectify things with her boyfriend. He had got fed up
with waiting for her to leave me and found someone else. I felt sorry for
myself and I think Paul felt sorry for me, so he never addressed the
surliness of adolescence towards me, as he might have done had Alice and I
stayed married. I got off very lightly in that respect.

'Alice thought I got off very lightly too. I took Paul on holiday. He had
been badly affected emotionally, his schoolwork had suffered and he was
pretty nervy, but we both came back more relaxed and restored, which
was not the case for Alice.

'I was paying all the bills and the mortgage and the rates but she was still
almost broke. She wasn't getting much work as an illustrator. She thought
I was having a great time. After all, when Paul came to me, we went out for
dinner, for treats, to films (there was no room to stay in the bedsit), so for
him, visiting his dad was exciting. Whereas home was boring. Home was
about changing socks and doing homework. Naturally Alice resented the
difference in how he saw it.'

When Paul was sixteen, Alice did marry her long-term lover and moved
to Ireland with him. Morris moved back into the old family home with
Paul.

'He had become a very surly adolescent, rejecting being mothered, but
still none of that was addressed to me because for a long time I had not
been responsible for his day-to-day discipline. He had used to mind
himself when he visited me (he still felt a little sorry for me), so I didn't
have to say "Don't" and "pick up those clothes". I didn't foster the view
that Alice was more at fault than me but I must have seemed like the good
guy.

'He also responded to the fact that I treated him as a person or a friend when I saw him, instead of as a child, which I would have done had I still been a live-in father. When I did move back to live with him, he felt more relaxed because there was only him and me. Alice's boyfriend had been living there for a while previously and tried to discipline him, which he didn't like.

'We had a terrific time. We were flatmates. I issued guidelines rather than directives, and this was deliberate. We did have disagreements sometimes, as flatmates do, but we both enjoyed discussing and solving things like two adults instead of the "because I say so" stuff.

'I loved the relationship. We were friends and drinking partners. He had lots of friends of his own but he always found time to go to films or sit and watch television with me. He wanted to.

'I feel really happy with the way that Paul has turned out. I think it was vital being honest with him at the time of the break-up. It was one of the few things I know I did right. But it was my wife who insisted on honesty in the first place. Left alone, I might have been tempted to sugar the pill.'

Three men had very sad and painful experiences as regards their children after their marriages were ended. Two, Dan and Philip, were in very similar circumstances. They were both in marriages that lacked real physical affection; both met, for the first time, women who offered them that kind of love and both were swept off their feet. In each case, their wives, whether very wounded or resentful or both, were unwilling to forgive and felt their husbands had effectively forfeited any rights to their children.

Dan, a warm large man approaching seventy with a surprisingly composed acceptance of his troubled life – he had been virtually rejected by his widowed mother as a boy and received many emotional knocks in his later life – said: 'The courts said I should see my son Matthew, who was ten, on Saturday or Sunday each week. But my wife prevented it. She would ring up at the last minute, saying he had to go to some event connected with school or something. She even told Matthew to tell the school that I was dead. That must have affected him but he appeared to take it in his stride.

'Sometimes months went by without my seeing my son. Friday nights were a torture because I was waiting for my wife to call and tell me the visit was off. She just said it and hung up. I think she enjoyed it. We could never speak to each other or discuss Matthew because she hung up.

'Sometimes, on weekends when she hadn't called, I would be waiting out in the road (I wasn't supposed to go into the garden) but Matthew wouldn't come out. Finally I thought, to hell with it, and went and rang the bell. No one was there.

'I worried about what my son thought of me. He was told derogatory things – that I had run off with a young girl, that I was weak and a liar. It hurt. I was afraid of asking too much because I didn't want to be appearing to probe and to put him in an uncomfortable position between his mother and me. So we ended up not really saying anythng about anything. I looked forward to those few visits so much and there we were, just standing in the Science Museum, nothing happening.

'Later things improved, perhaps because Matthew himself insisted on seeing me more. At sixteen, he came to live with me. His mother had never really stuck up for him or inspired him with any sense of his worth, whereas I went all out for him and I think that might have been why he came to me. I had married a woman, in his mother, who disliked men – just as my own mother did.

'Matthew is married now himself. He is very handsome and his wife is very pretty but they have decided they don't want children. I have often wondered if that was to do with his childhood.

'If a woman wants to make access difficult, there is no way to put that right. You can't refer to the court every five minutes. I resent what happened to me because it put an unnecessary burden on three people. The child runs between the parents, the wife is eaten by spite and the husband doesn't know where he is.

'It doesn't say much for love that it can change as violently as that.'

Philip's story had a less happy ending. He is a gentle man who is loath to make a bad situation worse, in this case for his daughter. He had been married for four years and his daughter was two when he met the first woman he had ever been strongly sexually attracted to. When he told his wife about his emotional dilemma, before starting an affair, she decided to divorce him.

'The court was generous in my access arrangements,' he said, 'but her family made the visits so tense that I found them almost impossible. My wife remarried and moved 200 miles away. I would make the trip down but I was only allowed to have tea with my daughter at the house, with my wife or her mother present. After forty-five minutes, they took her away. It was very very painful.

'I'm not a fighter and felt protesting would do no good, particularly for my daughter. I can't bear having to assert my rights and if human empathy isn't there, no legal arrangements can improve things. My ex-wife would accept no money from me and her husband wanted to adopt Katy but I refused. But, as my concern was that she was being properly looked after, I was relieved she had a stepfather and felt no resentment of him.

'She was three and a half when I last saw her. The last meeting I had was so unhappy for me and I also felt it may not have been any source of pleasure for the child. I felt that anyone could have taken her out and it would be the same to her as me. I wanted her to have an undisturbed upbringing and not to feel awkward about me. I was satisfied she had security and love from the family and I decided it was best in the long run not to see her.

'Also, I thought I might see my own path more clearly, though that may sound selfish. Katy meant so much to me that as long as I lived for those short meetings, which were acrimonious in actuality, I felt I couldn't re-build my life and confidence and be a comfort to her later, if wanted.

'I didn't tell my ex-wife I was stopping. I just stopped. I kept on writing to my daughter but I didn't say I wasn't coming anymore. She was so very small. Yes, maybe she doesn't understand why I stopped coming. I suppose I thought her mother would explain. I suppose I trusted her enough that she would give a fair picture of why.

'When I remarried a few years ago, I wrote and told Katy we would love to see her any time she felt like coming. But I have no hope or expectation of it while she is a minor. I don't think she will be allowed to though I hope that when she is seventeen, she might want to. She is now fourteen.

'She knows who I am. She writes to me about three times a year and I look forward to her letters enormously. But I am always disappointed by their quite understandable lack of subjective content. What she feels I don't know.

'I do worry about what she feels. I'm not into mysticism but I do have inclinations that way and therefore I consider that lots of feelings are not on a temporal level, which makes things better. On some level, I believe, she knows how I feel towards her.

'Knowing that I could ring and say I want to see Katy tomorrow makes me feel better than if the law had forbidden me access. But the law itself can't help anything where emotions and people are concerned. I wouldn't ring because I don't want to harm her life. I don't want her not to have her flute or her riding lessons or whatever because "daddy" is coming 200 miles today. No riding would mean deprivation and for what? What do I *really* mean to her in the end?

'I still miss her every day. I only feel free of that feeling when I am abroad and couldn't see her if I wanted to. I do hope I won't feel later that I made the wrong decision.'

Pete does fear he made the wrong decision. 'I wish I had left the door open,' he said. He left Pam when she told him of her affair with their

neighbour Roger, and Rober left his wife and moved into Pete's home four
days later. Pete was in a drowning state of confusion and fear, unable to
face what had happened or make decisions for the future and only conscious of feeling a total failure. He drank himself into oblivion whenever
he could.

'I was staying with my parents and came to take the children out on
Sundays. It went on for three months. One day I took the two of them to
the zoo and the elder boy said: "Do I call you dad or Pete and do I call
Roger dad or Roger?" I said: "I'll always be your dad" but I didn't answer
the question.

'After I dropped the kids off that night, I stopped the car and cried my
eyes out. Then I went and got pissed. I decided that the kids had a chance
of a stable home life with Pam and Roger and that I was the disruptive
element coming in and out. They were so confused! I decided to drop out.

'I went to see Pam and told her I wasn't going to see the children
anymore. She said: "I don't understand you at all" but I thought there was
a glimmer of triumph in her eyes. That suited her very well.

'I thought it was a tough decision to make but that I was strong enough
to handle it. There was so much emotion going round in my head that I
had to have something solid to base any decisions on. Not my feeling bad
or hurt, because decisions coming out of that would be harmful. The base I
chose was the welfare of the children. Every decision I made was about
"what is best for the kids?"

'I knew Pam would look after them. She was an extremely good mother
– loving, caring, firm. I told Roger that I would kill him if he hurt their lives
in any way. It was emotional but I meant it. And he has been a good father,
I know.

'I thought my decision was logical. Others say it was unnatural. I
thought I could handle it. I don't know if I did. I still cry, 15 years later.'

Pete carried on paying the mortgage and for the children until Roger
adopted them 18 months after moving in. 'I had decided to agree but I was
really mad and angry when I got the papers to sign, witnessed by a Justice
of the Peace. A social services man rang me at work and wanted to see me
about it. I said I didn't want to see him, I had made my decision. I didn't
like having to talk about my children because that made me upset.

'He told me to talk to him or he would subpoena me to court, where the
children could actually see me give them away. I saw him. He said, "Wouldn't
you like to say anything to your children? Would you welcome them if they
wanted to see you some time?" "Oh yes," I said. "Well, make a statement to
that effect!" he bawled at me. I did. I was grateful to him for that.

'I didn't feel animosity towards Pam till years later. I wrote and offered her and Roger money, with no conditions, for the children. She wrote back and said that I had never cared for her or the children during the marriage and now I was successful, I thought I could turn the clock back.

'I did used to wonder what the children looked like. If they were well. If they had got jobs. I'm desperately curious to know what they think about me. I suspect Pam would have turned them against me. I don't know that for a fact. But, in her mind, *I* left the children. I didn't have to, and I imagine she'll have told them that. I don't think she accepted my reasons. She couldn't have done it herself and nor could a lot of people.

'Yes, I wish I had left the door open. It does hurt me to think they might think I never cared about them. For my elder son's eighteenth birthday, I sent him a watch and a letter inviting him to visit me and my second wife. I got no reply. I don't even know if he received it or not. I can talk openly about the children to Sheila, my wife. She still reckons they'll get in touch. I don't think so. I try not to think about it.'

# =8=
# Children-
# living together

'I was very independent when my wife left. My parents offered to come over and help me with the children but I wouldn't have it. I made sure those kids looked immaculate and was proud of it.' Joe, an easy-going, big-hearted laboratory technician, had had a very conventional marriage until his wife became deeply depressed after their third child was stillborn, and started an affair. Joe had been the breadwinner, his wife the home-maker, until he arrived home one day to find his best friend in his bed.

He had been staying with a friend, in an effort to give a breathing space to the marriage so that they could start afresh. He was numbed by what he found, then decided to assert himself and move back into his home.

'She said, if I came back, she was leaving. She left me and she left the kids,' he said, speaking fifteen years later with no rancour at all. 'I chucked in my job (the man I had found in my bed was my assistant at work) and took the children on holiday for a week. I was still hoping that she would come back but she said no way. So I looked after the children.'

Thirteen per cent of single parent families are now headed by fathers. They are seen as special because of traditional ideas that children are better off with their mothers, a view still favoured by the courts except in special circumstances. Single fathers may therefore find themselves the object of outsiders' admiration and awe, if they are thought to be perform-ing their unusual role well, and may find themselves offered more help than the struggling single mother. Conversely, they may be looked at with suspicion and their every act scrutinised more closely by health or social service officials. However willingly men embrace single parenting when the need arises, they often still fear the effects on their children of mother loss and suffer more psychological difficulties in making the shift from part-time to full-time carers in a society where nurturing is dominated by women.

It happened that five of the men I spoke to had at some point brought their children up alone. Their experiences naturally varied according to their circumstances and attitudes.

For Joe, taking over the daily care of the family was automatic and instinctive, although his role till then had always been as earner and externally he appears to have a conventional view of male and female roles. Strong physically and mentally, he seemed to have no psychological problem in adapting.

'For the first few weeks, I looked after the children, who were two and four, on money I had. I've always been domesticated. I often cooked the Sunday lunch anyway and could cope easily on that side. But I didn't want to be stuck in the house all the time, brooding and on the dole. So I got an evening job as a debt collector. I put the kids on a mattress in the back of the van and they came too.

'I knew it was a dodgy thing, like, and I had to be careful. My job was to act aggressive and get people's money back but I couldn't afford to get laid out, with the kids in the back of the van! But I didn't have any difficulties and, in a way, it was a good thing because I was able to earn and I was also letting go of some of the aggression that I hadn't expressed towards my wife and my best friend.

'I did that for a year and then I got my job back as a lab technician. I took the children to school and found someone to collect them and look after them till I came back. The children missed their mother terribly but later she got in touch and started seeing them every other Sunday.

'It was knackering getting the children up, washing and feeding them, doing a full-time job and then doing all the washing at night. I appreciate what it's like for women who work and run families, it's a terrible strain. There's no time for play. But I took real pride in those kids. They always looked immaculate. About a year later, I met a girl where I was working. The children seemed to like her, although, if she ever stayed the night, I made sure the children were asleep. She started helping with the cooking and ironing and that did help a lot. Unfortunately, things didn't turn out as I expected at all when we eventually got married.'

Bill wasn't expecting to have the children to live with him when he and Louise divorced. Like Joe's wife, Louise had become severely depressed after a death in the family, her mother's, and also secretly began an affair. Bill was heartbroken that she wanted to end the marriage.

'We agreed she would stay in the house with the children, and I went to my mother's, who lives nearby. But within a couple of weeks, the three boys said they wanted to live with me. Louise's boyfriend had started visiting immediately after I moved out and the children didn't like it. I went and had a go at her about that and she stopped him coming round for a bit. But then she told the youngest boy that if she couldn't have her friends in, neither could he! What a thing to say to a seven-year-old! It was after that I decided to go for custody. The daughter, who was the eldest, decided to stay with her mother. I think she feels very pulled about it. She doesn't like the idea her mother might be lonely.'

Bill moved back into the family home. He is a very large, powerful-looking man, very stereotypically masculine, but he too had no psychological difficulty in adjusting to full-time caring. He is a self-employed painter and decorator and fits his hours round his children as much as he can. When he can't, his mother helps out.

'I love kids,' he said. 'I play games with them, whether they are mine or other people's. And I've always been domesticated. I love cooking, and cleaning and ironing are no problem to me. It was always me who bathed the kids and read them stories, that sort of thing, anyway.'

He is, however, very worried about the traumatic effect on the children. 'The eldest boy hates going to see his mother alone. He got there once and found Louise and the boyfriend kissing and cuddling and he ran home shaking. The young one will only visit her if I go too. I said to my wife, "Have you asked the children how they feel?" and she said, "They know that they can talk to me." But they can't. They are too upset to discuss their feelings with her at all.

'Louise knows they don't feel comfortable with her bloke there, and yet she never asks him to go out or takes the children out on her own. All the boys used to cry in their sleep and the youngest one wet the bed. But, now, nine months later, they are starting to be more open and loving again. My daughter is still with her mother but she spends a great deal of her time here. Her friends are in this road. She was here for the whole of the holidays and I don't think she really knows what she wants to do.

'The doctor suggested I take the children to see a psychiatrist after he learned that the young one was wetting the bed. The psychiatrist asked them a lot of things in front of me, like who did they talk to about any problems. They said me. He asked if I listened and helped and they said yes. He asked if I punished them when they were naughty and they told him I shouted. So the doctor asked me why I shouted and I said it got rid of my own frustration without hitting them.

'At the end he said that what I was trying to do for the kids was the right thing and no real harm could come to them while I was looking after them. It was a matter of time as healer.

'I do find it a strain bringing them up on my own. I get irritated about little things. I'll wash and iron and clean up and then they dirty everything and throw things anywhere, and I wonder, "Was it worth bothering?" I've got financial worries and I try to keep them to myself but sometimes I think it shows.

'Most weekends they have friends sleeping here, as many as four or five in sleeping bags over the place. I like letting them create their own environment and be natural about things. I joined Gingerbread, the one-parent family organisation, mainly for the kids, because they arrange all sorts of outings. I help organise things. It is also useful talking to other parents in the same position but I'm more the type who listens to others' problems, rather than talk about mine. I have two or three good men friends who will listen if I need to get things off my chest.

'At Gingerbread, there are quite a lot of women bringing up their families alone who feel very bitter now towards men. I think it is good that there are men there too, so that they can see we aren't all the same. Not all men put their families second.'

He smiles as he reveals the fact that he is seen as very eligible around where he lives. But although he gets invited to parties, and often goes, he isn't looking for a new relationship yet. He is all too aware of his children's feelings in that direction.

'I don't like being alone. I'm no different from anyone else. At night I certainly do miss adult and female company and I don't want to stay alone, but I don't think the children are ready for that, after the traumas they have gone through. At least I am older and can help them through their feelings, even if it does mean boredom for me.

'All the children went very quiet when the psychiatrist asked them how they would feel if I went out with another woman. Eventually they said it would be okay but they clearly weren't over-keen. A little while ago, we were at my mother's. She has got a rose-bush with the most beautiful colour roses and I picked a bud that I liked. One of my boys saw me and said: "What are you doing with that? You aren't giving it to some woman, are you?" He feels he wants all my attention. Even if I'm just talking to a woman neighbour at the gate, he'll find some reason to call me in for something.'

He feels that, in some ways, women have advantages when bringing up children alone, particularly in terms of support. 'When a woman is alone with her kids, other women in the same position call round to chat. But women wouldn't visit a man, obviously because they think that people will talk. So a man does tend to be more isolated.

'My neighbours don't treat me differently, however. I behave normally, have a laugh and a joke with them. I can ask for any help I need, such as sewing. But that is the only thing I don't do myself, so I'm not making constant demands on neighbours.

'I feel a lot of men would do what I have done, if put in the same position. I have realised that, though most divorced women round here say they love their children, they are very ready to leave them with baby-sitters and go out and enjoy themselves. They do that much more than men I know. If I go out, I take the kids with me.

'I think there can be a good side that comes out in divorce. Like, at Gingerbread, there are a lot of men who never used to do much with their children when they were a whole family. Now they are doing things they have never done before and seeing all the richness there is in being with children for the very first time. It is sad, of course, that it may take divorce to do that.'

Nick is unemployed. As he sits in his chaotic living room – he is trying to build some shelves – he has one expert eye watching all that his four-year-old daughter Dawn gets up to. He is twenty-seven.

'I can't work,' he says bitterly. 'With what it costs for a childminder, my travelling expenses, my rent, I'd come out with less than I have now on supplementary benefit. I used to work at a warehouse. If I'd carried on, I wouldn't have been able to get state help, so I had to stop. I'd much rather work. It's madness.' Nick's wife left him for another man and Nick was granted temporary custody of Dawn. Now his wife wants her back but, because Nick has already had her for two years ('an administrative bungle which meant permanent custody is only just coming up now'), he is hoping that he will be allowed to keep her.

'I definitely want Dawn. June was a good mother but she likes the good life and might bugger off again. When I was a kid, I was in a kids' home, so I want to make sure Dawn has a solid proper homelife. I found coping pretty hard at first. I knew nothing about nappies, but you just learn. She goes to nursery school, in the afternoons, so I do the housework then. June used to do all that. But I'm closer to Dawn now than I ever was before and so I'm lucky in a way. Not many fathers get that close.'

He is very angry about his legal situation. 'I could work part-time and still get some government help but it's the hours that makes it difficult. I can't find any part-time work anyway. I've thought of working illegally, even just to get money for Christmas, but if I got done I'd lose Dawn. I've got nosy neighbours.

'Dawn got offered some child photographic work but we can't even do that. Anything she earns would come off the social security. They don't even let you put it away for her when she is older, they say it is part of *my* income!

'I can't even take Dawn to see her mother. June's moved away now and it would cost eight pounds in fares. You don't get travelling expenses until the custody's settled.

'I think it's all wrong. If I remarry and my wife worked instead of me, June could claim part of that money if she had Dawn. But she has remarried and I can't claim maintenance from her husband. The law is biased against men. I've only got Dawn at all because of the blunder.'

A young man, full of nervous energy, Nick admits he gets very bored. 'I've lost contact with my friends because I can't go out. Even if I could, I haven't any money to go out with. I'd go barmy if it wasn't for the Gingerbread group and the playschool I take Dawn to. But I can't afford to get depressed too much because I don't want Dawn to see it. It is after she goes to bed that I think, "Oh God, I'm bored!" '

He also is aware that some problems he has don't usually face women. One that doesn't worry him, however, is the lack of a female figure to explain female things 'like periods and that. My sister lives right around the corner and so she can help that way a lot.' He does worry, though, that Dawn will feel awkwardly different when she goes to school.

'Suppose they all say, "Where's your mum?" It looks weird, doesn't it, living with your dad? That's how teachers seem to see it. They see you as a problem family. At playgroup, they are dead fast to notice any knocks or bruises – they think you've been beating her up. Once Dawn split her eye open on a table and they really questioned me. I don't think they would act quite the same if I was her mum.

'I had a social worker come round to see how Dawn was. She said she was going to check her for bruises and did it in front of me. I can understand their fear. But why did she have to do it so openly? Why couldn't she have done it discreetly while I was making tea?

'I think I get funny looks from women in the street. Most people think a mother should have a child. I've got nice neighbours next door but, further down, couples who are still married see me as a threat to their own security. They also think I lower the tone! They aren't nasty but now I'm not with June they don't bother with me. I'm bitter about that because now is the time I need people more.

'I expect to be lonely and bored for a long time yet. At the back of my mind, I know any girlfriend must like Dawn and Dawn can be very wilful and difficult if she wants. The only women I meet now are divorcees with children. They'd probably feel nervous about how I'd react to their child too. You've sort of got to fall in love with two people each.

'It does worry me sometimes that I might lose my temper with Dawn because of my own frustrations, or else end up spoiling her. But I think her life's okay. I've got more problems than she has.'

For all the admitted strains Joe, Bill and Nick have experienced, they came across to me as remarkably positive and confident about their roles as single parents. Their wish to look after their children was so strong that they had willingly re-organised their lives, giving up or changing their work styles to cope, and faced the consequences for themselves with considerable equanimity. Whatever bitterness they felt about being left by wives they all loved did not seem to sap their strength to face daily life. They had consciously and deliberately stepped out of 'role' whereas women in their position may feel less sense of choice, seeing it as their usual lot to be left with the baby. Not all men, of course, have the confidence.

Robert, the builder who was so humiliated when, in order to win custody, he had to recite how he had found his wife with other men, found it extremely difficult to cope with child-raising alone. At first, he was able to leave Mandy, his two-year-old daughter, with elderly neighbours while he went to work.

'But I was feeling so bitter and depressed. I had a massive chip on my shoulder about all women by then, so I had no female relationships at all. I was totally wrapped up in my work and Mandy. It was a mere existence. My health got worse and worse and then I got peptic ulcers. Then the old couple had to stop having Mandy because she became too much of a strain. Things just built up and built up and everything seemed loaded against me managing alone.

'I had no family, no friends and no contact with my wife. Someone else always collected Mandy for visits. I was trying to give Mandy a mother's love as well as a father's and I think it was a bit overpowering for her, as well as for me.

'Mandy started getting more and more upset whenever she had to say goodbye to her mother. It was very upsetting for me too. I spent a Christmas where Mandy and I were entirely alone and I was so miserable that, afterwards, I made the decision to give Mandy back to her mother and move out of the house.

'It was a terrible decision to have to make. But I felt by then that Mandy would be better off. At least my wife had a divorced sister who had children, so they could all help and be company to each other. I had no one and that meant Mandy suffered too.

'I left the house and went to stay with my sister 150 miles away in London. I didn't see Mandy for a long time. It was very painful but I just couldn't handle going back and seeing her, after leaving her. I also felt it would be bad for her to have me on the scene while she was readjusting to her mother. I don't know if that was wrong or right but I thought it for the best, regardless of my feelings.'

Later Robert and Mandy did resume contact and, years later, she came to live with him again. But it wasn't a happy period for either of them, partly because Mandy did feel that Robert had abandoned her and partly because of jealousy of and from his second wife.

Vicky left Canada and her mother Shelley, at the age of ten, to come and live with her father Jay in England. It is a continuing and very happy arrangement for both. For the previous six years, she had spent summers in England and herself decided that she wanted to go to an English school. 'And, of course, I used to spoil her whenever she was here, so she liked it,' said Jay. But the transition from seasonal to sole parenting was not initially comfortable.

'We had the most terrible rows for the first while and that worried both of us. We found we just didn't know how to behave with each other, now that the set-up was different. She resented my having to work and I felt guilty at not having more time. It went on quite badly until I got an au pair.

'I had a lot of learning to do myself. I was still only learning how to be honest with myself about myself. You can fake things with an adult, but not with a ten-year-old. We got over our difficulties when I started becoming more explicit about that *I* needed and how *I* felt. I had to admit my conflicts and stop feeling guilty over having less time than I or she would have liked, because of work.

'She didn't resent girlfriends but had strong opinions about them as individuals and let me know. It was worse in that respect before she was living full time with me. Once, one summer, she was absolutely awful to a woman I was involved with. But I think that was because I handled the situation badly. I didn't include Vicky properly because I felt guilty about her possibly resenting the relationship and that was silly, because it made things worse.

'When she started living with me, I did decide to keep the sexual side of relationships away from her. Either I would stay with the woman concerned or, if she did stay with me, I made sure Vicky didn't know. Why did I feel that was important? I suppose because I wouldn't talk even to close friends about what the nature of a new relationship was. I don't think it is their, or Vicky's, business. Also, it seems pointless to burden a ten- or eleven-year-old girl with that aspect, at a time when they are bursting with curiosity and fantasy.

'I did think it was a problem Vicky not having a mother figure on tap. She saw Shelley in the holidays but that isn't enough. I do have a lot of female friends and Vicky felt comfortable enough to talk to them about things. But, as she moved into puberty, it became more apparent that she needed some more stable figure. An au pair is too young.

'I also knew I wanted and needed to share the bringing up of Vicky with someone. Several months ago she covered herself up when I came into the room and I knew that it was the end of an era. I needed someone else around. If I hadn't met someone whom I am going to marry, I would have had to do something like share the house with a female friend who was committed to helping.

'Vicky is not resentful about my wife-to-be. She has been wanting me to have a regular relationship for some time and is ready for this one. I didn't even have to introduce the idea of marriage delicately. She was the one who said: "Why don't you two hurry up and get married?" '

Vicky is a lively, mature thirteen-year-old now. Jay is thankful that he learned, before it was too late, to share instead of shield her from his own needs and feelings as a father and as a man. He feels, too, that learning to relate honestly to a child has taught him much that is valuable in all his human relationships, particularly with women. As he found, it is less easy to be evasive about what he might feel or mean when dealing with a confronting child rather than with an equally evasive and emotionally defensive adult.

# 9
# Alone again

About half the men I spoke to are living alone, whether one year or twelve years after their divorce. The majority have had serious fairly long-term relationships since, most of which have failed to survive. Their attitudes towards themselves now and towards future re-marriage vary according to how each responded to a marriage that ended in divorce and what has happened to them after. Some feel that the experience, though painful, has opened them up and made them more confident of a successful lasting relationship to come; others have put up their emotional defences and declare themselves uninterested in long-term liaisons, albeit not always 100 per cent convincingly. Relationships with ex-wives and children also have strong bearing on how they face the future.

For Marcus, at forty-six now renting a room in a shared house, his feelings are a strong mixture of sadness and hope. He feels largely responsible for the breakdown of his marriage, because he was unable to admit to and share his insecurities, both personal and financial, as the head of a family, and because he rejected the idea of outside help until it was too late.

'I became very reclusive. I had always been a very social person,' he said, 'but I went through a period where I dreaded anyone coming round to the house or inviting me to a social gathering. Four years later, I still find it difficult to be with a lot of people because of a loss of confidence. I do find it is my inclination to gravitate towards people who have had a similar experience. If I meet someone who hasn't had a relationship so seriously break down, I wouldn't feel comfortable talking about being divorced. There is an inbred feeling of being socially unacceptable, even now. I do feel I have failed and that is what I have to live with.

'I instinctively feel I must make my way alone for a while, as I've relied too much on a female figure in my life. All my former attachments have in part been sparked in reaction to some loss. I met and married Rosalie shortly after a girlfriend of longstanding had left me; the girlfriend and I had set up flat together within weeks of my twin sister's emigration to Australia.

He looks at the framed pictures of his children that hang on the wall. 'I do feel lonely,' he admits, 'particularly when I am with the children and conscious there is only me with them. I also fear that, the longer I do go on being solo, the more difficult it becomes to get involved. Even if I get my full sense of identity back, I fear an inability to trust myself and my emotions.

'I see the dangers in being alone and being safe. I think that inevitably there will be problems for me in relating to someone else now. That is very sad and militates against everything that human beings are supposed to be – open, giving, caring. I should be very wary of someone new, although to live alone for the rest of one's life is a terrifying thought.'

He feels glad and relieved to have a workably amicable relationship with Rosalie, his ex-wife, especially for the sake of the children. 'But little things can spark off fierce resentments even now. If Rosalie isn't happy about something in her life, perhaps with her current boyfriend, she tends to take her frustrations out on me, I feel. I fiercely resent that because I know how prone I am to feeling guilty. I become enraged with her inside but I feel impotent because if I show my annoyance, I get my sins thrown in my face, and I'm back on the guilt trip. I have always found it hard to allow myself to be angry, although at least I now realise I have the right to be.

'I do feel in my heart that she gave up on our marriage too easily, although, on a logical level, I can be persuaded out of that. She was too preoccupied with her own problems to give due attention to the fact that I was in crisis too. But I have also realised in the past few months that I am more stubborn, self-willed and selfish than I would have liked to think. I like my own way and surprise myself at how deviously, emotionally, I go about getting it. Rosalie accused me of being manipulative and she is right. I am.'

It was only after marriage guidance, which he underwent alone and too late to save the marriage, that Marcus could acknowledge and express any of his deeper emotions. At the time he felt very strongly that the marriage could have been saved. 'Now I no longer have that yearning to go back to Rosalie. I know what we would have to go through to make it work and I don't want to have to do that right now. But I'm aware that, in two or three years time, when I would expect to have worked through most of the difficulties and resentments, both on my own and with her, I could want that very much.'

He does not see his divorce as all negative an experience. Preferable as it would have been for him to face his own emotional needs earlier, it was the crisis of marriage breakdown that brought him, through counselling, face to face with himself. 'It has undoubtedly been an opportunity for self development. I have discovered and learnt so much that makes sense of my experience of life, and I feel more in charge of it.' The book that caused him such angst because he couldn't bring himself to write it, got written, and well.

'I must have made up my mind that I had to do it, to prove to myself and to Rosalie that I wasn't completely a failure. I also forced myself to stick at teaching, even though I felt, "I can't do this. I can't stand up in front of a class and expose myself in this way." The whole experience, in fact, has cast a different slant on my teaching. Texts I thought I knew backwards I find myself reading as if for the first time. I let my own experience breathe life into what, to a student, is a dead text, and that has paid off terrifically in interest in my classes.

'I do feel I am getting happier. I am gradually getting the acceptance of myself that can lead to contentment. The children are a great source of happiness and joy, however painful the partings, and I'm more hopeful than not about a future relationship. I believe you just have to wait for the proper time for things to fulfil themselves.'

Also unprepared for another relationship yet is Bryan, the graphic designer. An extremely attractive, articulate man in his middle forties, who looks permanently as if he has just returned from a holiday in the sun, he went through a promiscuous period immediately after he split up from Cleo, 'because she had made me feel so totally rejected and unattractive.

'But even when I was playing around, I really wanted to find an important relationship quite quickly. I've been a bachelor and I don't want to go through all that again. But exceptional people are rare and so many are married.' He still seems very confident of himself, whatever insecurities may be below the surface.

'I went to singles parties – horribly predatory! So I gave those up. I planned to meet about fifty women, just to relaunch myself, but after twenty I abandoned the idea. I think it's easy enough to meet people. You just have to open yourself up. I put blinkers on for all the years of my marriage. When you take them off, there are plenty of people around.

'But I'm not actively looking now. I feel I must learn to be with myself before I can be with someone else. And I'm not ready for a decent relationship yet. I'm still bitter about my marriage not working and about the high settlement. I don't think any woman I'd like to meet would actually like *me* at present. I've got to do something about it – not just the bitterness but somehow getting Cleo to see that she ought to be making some contribution to looking after herself.

'I feel knocked sideways. I am at a point in my life where I would much rather be settled – although being settled can mean complacency and then the marriage breaks up. I have had girlfriends who have wanted more involvement but I was the one who didn't. I don't know if that is because I am psychologically still damaged or that I just didn't feel warm enough to them.

'Of course I would *like* an important girlfriend. I would like one today, whatever I say about it being too soon. If I meet someone, well and good. I have in my head someone *very* different from my wife. Someone with a good job but not hyper-ambitious, someone who can stand on her own two feet and respect herself enough to want to. Cleo was a very good journalist but she never bothered to write again, after the children.

'I feel the level of hostility is just as strong from her. But love and hate are both passionate feelings. Indifference must be the worst. Except, this way, the children do tend to get manipulated by us both and that isn't good.'

For all his resentment over footing a huge financial bill to keep his ex-wife as well as his children, Bryan lives in a very elegant flat, large enough to be a family home. He does harbour hopes of having another family. 'But a friend of mine, who is also divorced, has recently got involved with a woman who wants children and he says he can't face that again. He said to me, "Are you really so sure you want children again?" and although I said yes, I think I have to examine that more fully. Hitting sixty when the children are just into their teens is not the greatest of prospects.

'And another family will never replace the one that I have lost.'

Six men quickly became involved in heavy relationships which didn't have happy endings before finding that they feel more comfortable living alone, although they haven't shut the door on another long-term relationship.

It took Lew two very painful tortured years to become fully positive about himself again after he and Judy decided to call it a day. He had been pessimistic before marriage about their prospects; doubts and differences grew divisive and he ended up agreeing with Judy, their paths perhaps predictably having quickly diverged, to stay together till their daughter was six. By the time they parted, he was, he says, deeply depressed and 'personally and professionally incompetent.

'The failure of the marriage had just added to something that was there for me anyway,' he said. 'The fact that we had been so much at odds in terms of our ideas had left me unsure about who I was in everything. I'm very sure about where I stand now (ten years on) and I probably wouldn't have had that without that experience. The areas I mean span from politics to personal relationships.

'I didn't feel particularly worried about personal relationships after the divorce. But with the person I then lived with for four years, the pattern proceeded to repeat itself. We didn't marry but we ended up living together much quicker than we would have because we both had to move at the same time and Petra persuaded me it made sense to buy together.

'It was a bad time for her. Her father had just died very suddenly in a car crash and she needed emotional support. Otherwise I wouldn't have been in so deep by the time I realised that living together was the wrong thing for us to do.

'I thought Petra was more emotionally mature than she was. Large lumps of my personality are still at four years old and so, I discovered, were large lumps of hers. She had had a dreadful childhood which was very insecure and she made huge emotional demands that I couldn't cope with. Her emotional demands and my particular shortcomings in being emotionally expressive meant we didn't gell.

'I wanted things I wasn't getting too. I wanted assurance that she didn't need all of my attention all of the time. But she was very jealous and my reaction is to cut off, which made her upset. I know it isn't necessarily a good thing, to cut off, but it's what I do. I'm far happier talking about what's "out there" rather than me and relationships.

'Both Judy and Petra wanted a lot of attention, exclusive attention. I wanted companionship and affection but also someone who would be able to enjoy being with other people, expanding our horizons.

'Petra wanted to marry. She felt insecure and said she *needed* the status of marriage. But I couldn't marry again. I felt it would be humbug. I thought it would be better if she worked out the need, instead of cosseting it by marriage.

'I am definitely happier now. What makes me happy? All sorts of things, from work going well to a lovely sunset yesterday to having a nice meal with someone tomorrow. I'd be foolish to say there are no emotional gaps. I think, because of my upbringing, which was oppressive, and then my mistakes later, the gap I feel most is not having developed my capacity to maintain and develop relationships at many different levels. Because of circumstances I've got into, and my reaction to those circumstances, I've actually blocked relationships. No, I haven't considered therapy. I feel it is a skills problem, rather than a personality one and all I can do is keep practising.

'I am talking about all relationships, not one-to-one. I feel one-to-one relationships are highly overrated. They can be useful things to have but the need to maintain one for a long time is more to do with giving children stability and making life hassle-free than about real need.' And then he is off, talking in the generalities which he finds most comfortable. 'Extended families, where there are bossy aunts and grandparents, can be extremely oppressive. Whereas nuclear families are plain nutty. They don't provide the necessities of life – experience for the young or support for the old. Surely there has to be something in the middle?'

Lew is jolly and sparkly and his large brown eyes are full of the warmth he eschews expressing. 'Some people are fortunate to meet someone they feel easy with in all situations,' he shrugs. 'I haven't. But that possibly reflects contradictions in my personality. I behave in very different ways with different people – almost random repertoires of behaviour.

'The main thing I have learned from my relationships is that I and most people are more subject to programming instilled in us, about marriage and commitment, than I had ever been willing to realise. I felt duty bound to commit myself to both Judy and Petra, and I couldn't act rationally to stop it. An awful lot of probing goes on, to challenge old ideas of relationships, but we still react from the ideas we received about marriage from parents in the first place.

'Would I marry again? Press the right buttons and anything can happen. So much that is fundamental is on automatic pilot – and that's very worrying, isn't it?'

The fear of repeating the same mistakes in relationships is very often grounded, partly, as Lew says, because fundamental ideas about marriage and commitment don't always change, even in the light of experience. A person may unconsciously seek a partner who was like a parent and that pattern repeats itself in each successive relationship until it is worked out. Some therapists say that, even if the chosen partner is not like the opposite sex parent or previous partner, in behaviour or attitude, we will project that image on to them, by interpreting their behaviour to fit the type we are accustomed to, or we will subconsciously set about creating the relevant behaviour patterns in them by manipulating or controlling our own.

Dick, who found his next big relationship repeating the pattern of his marriage to Ruth, wonders: 'Is it that I am attracted to insecure women or that *I* bring out the insecurities in them?' He is inclined to accept it may well be the latter, as he didn't realise Eleanor, his girlfriend, was at all insecure when he met her, and consciously was looking for someone confident and independent in a way that Ruth was not.

Unlike those mentioned so far, he did not feel 'bruised or guilty' in the aftermath of his failed marriage to Ruth. 'The marriage had to end. But that didn't make me feel that I had better not get into another relationship or I would get hurt,' he said.

When he met Eleanor, the first attraction was a strong sexual one. But she also, in his eyes, had the same kind of innocence that had attracted him to Ruth and even a similarity in features. The relationship seemed different, however, because whereas he had felt with Ruth that he had played a 'teacher' role, Eleanor had interests in her life which she introduced him to. Very quickly it became intense.

Then the familiar pattern emerged. Eleanor wanted more attention than he was willing or able to give and the more he withdrew, the more insecure and emotionally demanding she became. 'It turned out that she had more insecurities than Ruth. I had thought that she was interested in her career – she was training to be a photographer, having worked till previously as a teacher – but I had failed to see that, in fact, our relationship was everything to her and that her own life ceased to be important. It was back to the same syndrome where everything revolved around us.

'I detached myself less from the problems this time. I was able to talk much more about them, to see them coming and face them. But I certainly wouldn't have got involved with her if I could start over again. It is so difficult to communicate when a situation is so emotionally charged.'

His son Tim was also a source of stress to Eleanor. 'She desperately needed to be liked by him – and was. But I think she felt jealousy because Tim represented a bond between me and Ruth.'

Dick feels he has learned from his repeat performances. 'My pattern has been that I get very intensely involved at the beginning of a relationship and bring the person with me, then reach a point when I have to withdraw to compensate. Now I think I'm a little more objective, a little less intense at the start and, hopefully, therefore, more able to retain some intensity in the middle.

'But I don't think I do want to spend my whole life with anyone. I need time alone. From my experience of women I have been attracted to, they have needed a lot of attention, so now I feel it is unlikely that any woman could allow me necessary space, although that is generalising just from what happened to me.

'I am looking for emotional relationships where there is a closeness and real involvement but not necessarily where I spent the rest of my life living with one person. It is unlikely I would marry again, as I don't want to live with someone and I don't want another child. And I would never marry because a woman wanted security again. Ruth had needed that and Eleanor had wanted it too.'

He is aware, however, like Lew, that perhaps the right buttons only need pushing and he will find himself pitching in all over again. 'I don't expect to meet someone with whom I can have a blissful relationship. But somewhere in the back of my mind there is still this feeling that it *could* happen. I had felt that about Eleanor at first.'

For all that he has said, he claims that he hasn't put up emotional defences against the future. 'As a result of my marriage, I feel I can let my guard down *more* in relationships. I feel less emotionally vulnerable. It's like jumping out of a plane with a parachute. The first time you don't know if you can survive. The second time, you know your feet will hurt – but you do survive.'

It is not a view that is commonly shared. However destructive it may be in a new relationship to keep feelings back through fear of hurt, that tends to be the initial reaction to the emotional bruising of divorce followed by another failed relationship. Steve is a case in point. He had married at the age of twenty-two and it was a great shock to him when, three years later, his wife had an affair. She refused to give the man up and so he very quickly sent her divorce papers to sign, in which he appeared to have had an affair with a Miss X 'just to get it over with quickly'.

Despite the fact that his trust in his wife had been destroyed, he didn't feel less trustful of women generally. 'I had had a very stable family background and I tended to trust everyone,' he said. 'My confidence wasn't completely shattered, therefore, and I was open to a new relationship.' He met Anne very shortly after his divorce and they moved in together only two months later.

'It didn't seem particularly quick to me at the time. It seemed more like an adventure. I had been very down and depressed and I sort of felt it didn't matter whatever I did then. Who the hell cared? I thought I loved her. She was the only person who showed any sympathy and love and I became wrapped up in that.

'I wanted to marry her, but she thought marriage was a waste of time. That bothered me. It seemed not to make sense. Not marrying seems to me like not being willing to accept a responsibility to the relationship.

'We started having terrible rows, which I hate. They seem so futile. She felt I was away too much because of my job. It was true but there was nothing I could do about it. She had known what she was getting into.

'I'm not sure what led to the actual break-up, except in the end I couldn't do anything right. If I put a cup down, she'd see malice in it. I felt I couldn't carry on living like that and I left.

'Now I *am* shaken about relationships. I don't trust anyone anymore. I look on stable people as very rare instead of as the norm, but that's probably distorted too. What's a stable person? Someone who doesn't expect too much out of life, someone who makes things happen and gets on with it.

'I'm not the slightest bit interested in relationships right now. I'm actively avoiding them but I suppose it won't last. If I do have another, I'll be more suspicious, less trusting. Perhaps my relationships have been unsuccessful because I'm too easy-going, instead of trying to take charge of what's happening. I've got to stop being so worried about rows. If I do feel something, instead of keeping it to myself, I've got to learn to say it, even if it means I get a saucepan thrown at me.

'I have the same ideals about marriage as I always had. Two people should want each other exclusively, otherwise there's no point in being married. I seem to have morals and ideals which are very old fashioned to other people, but I'm not prepared to change them.'

Steve doesn't think Anne was similar in personality to his ex-wife. The patterns he has started to see are those established by himself and his own behaviour in relationships, whereas the responses of the women have been different. Donald, however, has become alarmingly aware that the kind of insecurity he found cloying in his wife comes out in himself when involved with a stronger woman.

His wife Joanna, had wanted a settled suburban existence in a nice house with children, against all of which his restless spirit rebelled. He saw her as becoming more and more insecure and emotionally demanding. 'Even sex became an exercise in reassurances, not enjoyment,' he said.

When they split up, still childless, he quickly became involved in another relationship which lasted five years. He had felt a need to fill the emotional void that followed his divorce but was looking for someone very different from Joanna. He may have suffered from a syndrome commonly seen by marriage guidance counsellors: so keen a determination to avoid repeating old patterns that it leads to overdosing in the opposite direction. Donald said of his next lover:

'She was a strong, ambitious woman who didn't want marriage. We lived separately and the relationship was much more independent. She liked doing crazy things and exploring places, so we had a lot in common,' he said. On the surface, it seemed, he had found himself a perfect match. 'But she was much stronger and brighter than I am. She was very much a modern woman and I suffered from feeling insecure in that. I was the one demanding the reassurance now and she didn't feel it necessary to give it.

'I felt jealous and possessive about her. I found her independence difficult to cope with, although she was actually a very loyal, committed partner. After five years we were taking up a lot of each other's social life but I still wasn't getting the reassurance I thought I wanted. So I reached the point of wanting to explore other people and other opportunities. She was not getting what she wanted either and took that opportunity to suggest separation.

'I wanted her back, once it was over. Emotionally it was very hard for me to come to terms with because, like a little boy, I wanted what I couldn't have and it was very compulsive.

'Of course I felt the boot was on the other foot. And it happened again in another traumatic relationship. The woman was so extraordinary that I became infatuated and obsessed. I couldn't get her to do anything except what she wanted to do and our collective happiness was greater if I did what she wanted, because her agony was extreme if I didn't.

'We spent all our weekends at her place, which reveals something, I think. Sex was minimal because she didn't really enjoy it and didn't need it for reassurance. Whereas, with her particularly, I needed sex as reassurance as well as for enjoyment. I didn't get it, yet the relationship was still compulsive. Fortunately she went to work abroad so the relationship was ended for me.'

Donald is now a suave and philosophical forty. He remains convinced that his early frustrated battles for independence from his mother as an eldest son are much to blame for his inability to settle for the safe without feeling smothered while at the same time feeling insecure when not in control. He now prefers to spread himself more thinly.

'I think it is easier to do a wide variety of things with a wide variety of companions. I know a number of independent women, several divorced, who like the idea of a non-committed relationship. But there are also those who would really like to settle down, as well as single ones who are still working out where they are about sex. They may say they only want a sexual relationship if we are having a committed monogamous relationship. But I say that means we are on a conveyor belt to seeing if we should settle down, and I don't want to. Settling down is a difficult thing to choose to do, if you don't need it. I can cope running my life and home quite happily without a woman.

'I think I prefer a wider range of people until or unless I find one woman I'm prepared to make sacrifices for. The sacrifices would be giving up a lot of my single women friends. Partners are never really happy about people you have slept with in the past. It's a hard one to sort out. I think I would be jealous of ex-lovers too.'

Having been both sides of the fence, the object of a woman's insecurity, and insecure himself, he feels insecurity may be an unpleasant inevitability for one or the other. 'I think it is difficult for neither party to feel jealous or insecure if a relationship is a long one. It only works in relationships where partners have fixed routines and don't look at these issues. But, if you are a free-thinker and have an exploring nature, the emotions are more difficult to manage.

'The two women who followed my wife both felt that, if you are not in a marriage, you don't have the right to ask questions. But that creates a communication gap. Whereas in marriage, it is taken as read that you can ask questions. And the problem is you may no longer be interested in the answers.' Like Dick, he yearns for closeness without commitment.

Donald's dilemma is a familiar one. Men who are seen as leaders and individualists, effective in their work and in taking control, often attract and then feel stifled by more dependent women. But only when they consciously seek someone of similar spirit do they come up against their own dependency need, all the more threatening for its unfamiliarity and sometimes potentially devastating.

Charles became extremely confused and insecure when he found himself dealing with a woman who was more strong-willed than his wife. He had been having an affair with Maria for several years before the break-up of Maria's marriage led her to pressure him to leave his own. It was agreed, by him and his wife Deborah, that he should move out until he decided whether he wished to return wholeheartedly to his marriage and children or opt for divorce. He took a small flat.

'Maria had hoped that I would move in with her but I found myself unwilling for quite a few reasons. The main reason was my children – I felt I might lose them if I did. But I also discovered that I didn't trust Maria. I was unconsciously aware that she was unreliable and possessive and would make my life very difficult. I wouldn't have been so free to pursue my business, which entailed some travel. Deborah had always accepted that part, however she felt, but Maria definitely wanted a family man. I felt frightened of becoming possessed. Her children were considerably younger than mine and I also didn't feel I wanted to go through fatherhood again, for hers.'

A businessman capable of making decisions in his work, Charles found himself incapable of making any in his emotional life. Eventually all decisions were taken for him. Maria lost patience and they didn't see each other for a couple of months, during which time she met someone else. Deborah, meanwhile, having seen no change of heart, decided she wanted a divorce.

'When everything was over, I felt devastated,' he said. Despite his now admitted reservations about living with Maria, he had convinced himself at the time that he was only waiting for his divorce to be properly agreed and settled before committing himself to her. 'I had left Deborah on the basis that I had someone else in my life whom I intended to marry, and I ended up with no one.

'My world fell apart. It has taken me six years to adjust emotionally, to reach a point where I feel I would be capable of marrying again, free of the emotional impact of the break-up. Now I feel I would like to meet someone and settle down. But, if I don't, I have quite a good life on my own. I have lots of friends, both men and women. I have a few comfortable sexual relationships, where all we both want is sex and friendship. I certainly wouldn't be so happy if I didn't have that.'

He feels his criteria for a marriage have changed since his first. Of greatest importance would be common interests 'which I lacked with Deborah'. He would want the relationship to be sexually strong and monogamous and, like Donald, accepts that he would probably have to lose the friendships he now has with other women, not just the sexual component of them. Career would take much more of a second place because he now sees a good relationship as more important.

His children are grown up and living their own lives away from home, but he still sees Deborah. 'I had dinner with her only last week. We are on good terms but not close, because we have so little in common.' He thought for a moment. 'If *she* remarried, I would feel a qualm or two. Not sexual jealousy but, well, I suppose I would feel I had lost her. Isn't that strange?' he laughed.

Malcolm the printer felt no such qualms about his ex-wife's remarriage. 'She has got herself a much better fellow than me – certainly better-looking!' he says, a comment which is meant as neither flip nor sarcastic but reflects the slight chip he has about his own conviction that he is not an attractive man.

He hadn't felt that marriage was a very good idea and accepts quite philosophically that he and his wife drifted apart and amicably decided to go their separate ways.

'When I got divorced, life went on much as before because I stayed in the family home and the children were over to see me whenever they wanted. Their attitude towards me didn't seem to change. I missed the family around me but not to any great extent. I think I'm a person who shouldn't have married till later in life. Now, at fifty, I feel I could appreciate young children and a young wife in her twenties. I would like to have got married at forty-five.' He finds he is only attracted to much younger women.

Quite shortly after his divorce he met a girlfriend who was with him for the following nine years. 'I've never been an attractive man, so I have always had to work at getting women. I'd always maintained men friends through my marriage but instead of seeing them once a week in the pub, I'd see them more often. One was very attractive to women and the women would have friends whom I met. People talk as if you have all the choice in the world but you can't have a relationship with someone who doesn't want you.

'My girlfriend, Caroline, had her own place and she was a workaholic like me, so in some ways we were well-suited. But the relationship recently petered out. She is 20 years younger than me. Age wasn't a problem, except that she started wanting more from a relationship whereas I, as an older man, now want less. The older I get, the less compromising I get. I resent wasting time on anything I don't want to do.

'She always wanted to be forward planning and pressuring me into commitments. I just want to jog along. I feel both sadness and a relief that it's over. It was inevitable, anyway.

'We used to have problems over my children. She reacted badly to them and felt jealous about my spending money and time on them. I felt pulled two ways but I always took the kids' side because of the guilt and responsibility, I suppose. But I know that made it harder for my girlfriend.

'I'm quite happy living alone. A lot of my bachelor friends always have and I have plenty of men friends for companionship. I have enjoyed life a lot so far and every year gets better because I have more and more financial independence and can do what I want to do. A good relationship would be nice but I don't think about it much. I just go from day to day. I certainly don't see the point of getting a divorce and then getting married again straight away. I mean, if the divorce happens because you don't like the state of being married, it seems ludicrous to get back into it.

'Most men I know are happy, whether they are married or not. But most women I know are verging on discontented and looking for something better. Maybe it is in their nature. They seem to want more out of life. Men just jog along.'

Little seems to disturb Malcolm's calm or alter his laid-back acceptance that all has been for the best but then again, he wouldn't have let me know. 'I'd say divorce has worked out well for both of us. I don't regret it at all and my ex-wife's much better off now. It has been very positive. Divorce isn't all gloom and despair. It can mean moving on to better things. All my friends are much happier with their second wives.

'I think it is natural these days that you'll have more than one deep relationship in your life. People are not likely to marry at twenty and stay together till seventy. Children are the only tragedy of the thing. And yet I don't believe broken marriages always screw up children. I think you can be screwed up by good marriages too. You are over-protected and have a false sense of security.'

As Malcolm himself admits, his experience of marriage hasn't changed him. He admits to being dogmatic and unwilling to change and can only imagine a relationship for himself working right if a woman is prepared to fit in entirely with his lifestyle. Failing that, he would rather be alone, and considers that highly likely. 'I'm not the sort of person who is open to talking about feelings much,' he said.

Angus too shies away from the deeper kind of emotional commitment that requires significant compromise. His reaction to years of playing the supportive role to his manic-depressive and suicidal wife Claire has been to become much more protective of his own personal space and freedom. He had a number of short, uncommitted relationships after the marriage broke up.

'I was happy about my freedom. I did see the women I met as people, not just bodies, but I didn't want to be committed to them. They tended to want more from the relationships than I did, but I was scrupulously honest, I didn't spin any lies. I just wanted a good time without strings attached.

'I went around saying that marriage as an institution was dreadful, then I mellowed and just said that it wasn't for me. It still isn't for me.'

Six years later, he does live with a girlfriend in a flat they own but he doesn't believe that the arrangement will be permanent. 'Living with someone is different because there is no long-term commitment. It's that bit of paper that does it. Wendy and I have a legal document setting out what will happen financially when we part and that's it. Not that our parting will be any the less sad, though.

'It works well at present. We have a lot of things in common but we also live our own lives and have our own friends. I suppose I do love her. I think I'm more in touch with my feelings than I was but I don't know for sure. I feel we have both revealed a lot of ourselves to each other but she says she still feels she knows very little about me.

'I think I do hold on to bits of myself. The experience of my marriage has done that. It has made me less happy about giving myself. I have faced up to my own needs and I know I'm not a saint, so I am more wary of giving up my needs for someone else's. Is that good or bad? It just happens to be the case.

'I don't regret my marriage. Once the divorce was through, I felt I had survived a big experience, like surviving a first parachute jump. I felt enriched somehow.

'I don't think Wendy and I will be together for life. I think she will change, want more, and she would like children. I don't now. It is selfishness and fear of commitment. I cannot see myself wanting to change my life so radically.

'I don't know whether I see myself alone in old age. I haven't faced it. If it happens, it happens,' he said. For the present he considers himself happy enough and is generally optimistic about life. The path he has chosen is one that feels comfortable to him.

Three men who are still living alone feel that the self-knowledge, however painful, that they have derived from marriage has enabled them to raise their expectations and alter attitudes towards another relationship. They, unlike Malcolm and Angus, are highly hopeful that this time it could work.

When Jeff the architect split up from Kay a few years ago, he experienced about ten months of difficult readjustment. 'It was a slow progressive degeneration. I was missing the children, fighting over legalities and was so pre-occupied with the separation that I couldn't concentrate on work, so then I ended up with money problems too.

'It felt bad to me to be single when everyone else was a couple. I didn't like going out alone. I also felt a conflict of need because I wanted to meet women but, psychologically, I didn't want to get involved and I personally find it hard to have superficial relationships. I had personal therapy, which helped me a lot, and also a couple of good friends who would listen. It was a very new experience for me, being so needy to talk about myself.

'A year later I met Chrissie. I was ready for a new relationship but not for marriage. I also wanted someone who could do things with me and the children. It didn't seem right to take casual girlfriends along. It hasn't been problem-free in that respect, however. My younger daughter sees Chrissie as competition and both children can sometimes be off-hand and rude to her. But I suppose that is inevitable.

'I know Chrissie wants marriage and children. Last year I couldn't have contemplated that, now I can but not immediately. I would rather my children grew up a bit more first, although Chrissie may not be prepared to wait. I'm aware it's a repeat of an old problem. Chrissie wants children now and I want to wait, just as was the case with Kay. But I just know that, whatever I do now, the outcome will be so much better. In marriage I am now aware of the need to work through things right from the beginning, not leave them to drift. I am much more capable of understanding others' emotional needs and feel more willing and able to meet them. I feel very hopeful for the future,' he said.

Neal, the ebullient artist whose wife had been anorexic, feels that, after two years of therapy, he has become capable for the first time of an honest relationship. In therapy he discovered how much he had been bound in his life by a sense of duty and self-sacrifice, inculcated in him by a religious family upbringing. He discovered a deep distrust of women, stemming from his distrust of his mother. The sense of duty led him to go through with a marriage he already knew was wrong for him; the self-sacrifice got twisted into selfishness and the distrust of women meant his pattern was to entice and then 'run a mile', in the several short relationships that succeeded his marriage.

'I have, over the past year, gradually become closer and closer to someone and we are likely to live together now. I would consider marriage because I'm not frightened of the concept involved. But I wouldn't marry her whole family. I feel that family, the social machine that masquerades as a support mechanism, is the most dangerous thing about marriage. It sets out to make you conform and never supports doubts or helps you examine alternative ways of living. I have a horror of families as a result of my first marriage.

'I wouldn't allow my relationship with Pauline to be affected by her relations or mine. They will have to understand that we are separate from them, that we are not becoming part of a network of inter-dependence and inter-responsibilities that seem expected when you marry.

'I no longer see marriage as a life-long commitment. I think that blights its chances anyway. With Pauline, it is the quality that counts,' he said.

Neal is forty-two and Pauline is thirty-six. He has had to confront the problem that Donald and Charles both anticipate – the difficulty of retaining or letting go of long-standing friendships with single people of the opposite sex. 'In view of our ages, we both of course have a number of friends of the opposite sex,' he said. But he and Pauline do not plan to give up their separate friendships. 'Yes, I do get jealous sometimes if she sees some man friend of hers without me, even though I know there is nothing sexual any more. If I get jealous, I tell her and we talk about it.

'The same applies for her. I can be irresponsible and live for the moment and then try to live it down later. I could conceive of being seduced into bed by a former partner. But Pauline is more responsible. If she wanted to go to bed with someone, it would be because of their worth or something I'm not giving her. We've agreed to keep all this sort of thing in front of us, to face it instead of avoid it,' he says.

It all sounds very adult. 'Adult? Or dull?' he suddenly wonders and is off into artistic reconstruction of his past. 'All that jangling discord of youth, with its counterpart of stunning harmonies, sometimes you miss it. But I am forty-two, and this time it is going to work.'

Relationships are definitely worth work as far as Tony is concerned. Having married young to escape the tightly drawn net of his Italian family and then found, when already a father, that he hadn't experienced enough of life or women or adventure, he had looked more and more for stimulation outside the home. He didn't have affairs, although he would have liked them, and was shocked when Beth, his wife, did – and wanted to end the marriage. It was only afterwards he came to appreciate what he had lost.

'For two years I couldn't come to terms with being away from the family situation,' he said. 'I became introverted and unsociable and spent the time going through my feelings. I experienced all the feelings I was capable of feeling about the children, Beth, what I had done with my life.

'I realised that I had married too young and fallen into it thoughtlessly. I realised that the way you treat people is the most important thing in life. My behaviour had been so negative in my marriage. I hadn't had the positive side of my character working for me at all.

'Even now I think that, if I had been more positive, honest and straightforward a person, I would still be happily married to Beth.

'I thought about what love is. I had never thought about that in marriage, never told her I loved her, never really showed it. Ridiculous! I still do love her.

'Looking back, I think that family life is almost a good enough reason for existence in itself. There's enough of substance in it. But I got involved with an imaginary world outside.'

After two years spent dwelling on his mistakes, Tony was fortunate enough to snap out of his introspection. 'I woke up one morning and realised I was vegetating. I had been over and over everything and saw myself becoming obsessed and self-pitying. Literally, that morning, I decided that I would meet a lady when I left the house. And, like magic, while waiting at a garage for something to be fixed in my car, I met a girl who was also waiting. We got chatting, went for a coffee and I asked her out that evening.

'From that time on, I decided to get out and meet people and forget my problems. I joined evening classes and generally put myself about.'

The relationships he wanted at that time were fun, quick, fairly superficial ones. 'In the end, they weren't satisfying but I wasn't looking for satisfaction. I wanted a variety of experiences with people looking for the same.' Since then he has had two serious relationships which have helped him assess unrealistic wants and real needs.

'I met a woman with whom I fell madly in love, perhaps for the first time, because the feelings were so different from when I married Beth. I had always fantasised about an incredible romance and this was it! The being in love was the be-all and end-all of our relationship, extremely stimulating and exciting but totally unrealistic. With her, I thought about making love or being in love the whole time. I was extremely upset when she ended it. It was as if the caravan of dreams had arrived and then been taken away again.

'Since then, I have had my best relationship yet, with a very special woman called Kathryn. It wasn't especially physical or sexual and there was no mention of love, yet the relationship was one of mutual independence and affection. It was good being with each other. Whereas with the other girl, making love was the heart of the relationship, with Kathryn it was part of a whole.

'She is an incredibly lively, energetic person without any hang-ups. It was easy to let her take the lead and then I found that left me feeling excruciatingly vulnerable. There are certain things in myself I need to develop, like leading instead of just being taken along, and so we are now just friends. But *real* friends, which I wasn't with the other one, or my wife.

'I now think friendship should be the basis of a relationship. It is the enduring thing. I would quite like to have another family and I know I would be different. I have changed enough and discovered enough about me to make it work. I have been alone and I would prefer not to be. Relationships are definitely worth the work.'

According to research, he may well have his priorities right. An American study of 300 couples still happily married after at least fifteen years, showed that, for both men and women, considering their partner as their best friend and liking them as a person were the top two reasons given for why their marriages survived.

# 10
# Second marriage

Men who say of marriage, 'never again' are definitely in the minority. As many as a third who remarry do so within three months of divorce or certainly within a year and not only if they have left their wives for another woman. Men tend to remarry more quickly than women, perhaps because, for most, the emotional burden of being exiled from the family is heavier than the financial burden of divorce. (For many, the financial burden may lighten if the second wife also earns an income.) Being alone is more than many can handle, with any happiness.

Research shows that people who embark on second marriages usually have more realistic expectations. But a good many, particularly men, rush in with little understanding of why the previous marriage went wrong and unwittingly ready to repeat the whole traumatic process. More second than first marriages end in divorce.

Pete, who made the hard decision to stop seeing his children, on the grounds that he was the disruptive element in their lives, feels he has been very lucky that his second marriage has worked so successfully. He married a year after his painful divorce from Pam, who, in turn, quickly married the neighbour with whom she had had an affair.

After breaking up with Pam, Pete went through several months of misery and disorientation, feeling he was a total failure and capable only of immersing himself in drink. He turned to sex for reassurance. 'There seemed to be a lot of women at work who wanted a fling and I was only too happy to provide it. I started to feel a bit like a playboy. It felt wonderful, women actually wanted my company as well as my body. It was a stroking I badly needed.' His self-esteem as a male was totally in tatters, sexually and psychologically.

But, he remembers, he had little time for other people's feelings, wrapped up as he was in his own. 'I was brutally honest. I'd say to a woman,

"I can't see you Friday. I'm seeing someone else." I felt I could handle no more lies. But I wasn't treating women well at all. One time I went out with a woman while the divorce was going through. I was going to get pissed and she didn't want me to. She kept reminding me I was driving. I ordered a double whisky and then ordered her a taxi, saying "If you want to be with me, you're with me on *my* terms." I was so dismissive.'

Pete met his second wife Sheila two months after he had left Pam. 'She was simply one of a number of women I knew. Then we went out together and the third time we went out we had a good talk. I said "I like you and I don't want to hurt you" and she replied, "I usually say that."

'I wasn't nervous of another relationship. I didn't care what people thought of me because they couldn't think worse than I did myself, so I could take risks. I couldn't be hurt any more than I'd been already hurt, I felt. In a way, it's like being dead. You stop feeling pain. But although I wanted everyone to love me madly, I didn't want to give back all of myself.

'When Sheila got fed up and said she didn't want to see me anymore, all I could think of was seeing another girl that evening. But then she got upset, so I stayed.

'Sheila saved my life at that time and it was exactly right to marry when we did. But I remember analysing very coldly whether we were suited. Does she scream and argue (I couldn't have stood that again), does she like the same things, is she comfortable with herself? We both felt an equal need to receive, and a want to give, love and strokes and attention. We have had a 13-year love affair. We both respect each other and never put each other down.'

When Pete met Sheila, he already had a long legacy of feeling small, inferior and inadequate as a person because Pam, he says, continually put him down. It is a feeling which unexpectedly can still confront him now. 'Last weekend I had to be abroad on work. I didn't know anyone. I could have got a coach tour somewhere but all the old inadequacy surfaced. The old "what am I going to do? where am I going to go?" that was so crippling after I left Pam. I couldn't leave my room and just felt bad and lonely. Yes, I could have put on my clown outfit or my playboy outfit but a tiny person is hiding inside, crying "I'm hurt!" or "I'm lonely." '

Despite the fact that he was wearing the playboy outfit when he met Sheila, and outwardly appears strong, good looking and confident, she, he says, was astute enough to realise his need for reassurance, particularly as regards her attraction to other men. He had during his marriage felt badly humiliated by Pam's open flirtations at parties.

'I thought Sheila was looking at another man in a restaurant once, and I went berserk. In fact, it was a mistake and I believed her. She had been miles away but I thought she was looking at the bloke at the next table. She was very understanding and reassured me. She didn't say "fuck off", like Pam would have done.

'At the beginning of our relationship, after that incident, she went out of her way to reassure me that I was needlessly jealous. If we went to a party, my instant defensive reaction was "Oh, I know what's going to happen here." But she would stay by my side and refuse dances. Once I felt reassured, we were both able to relax. I knew she wouldn't humiliate me when she did dance with someone.

'It can still happen, of course. Even now, if I knew a particular man would bed her if he could, I don't like her talking to him. I suppose it is fear that Sheila will find him attractive too. Something triggers this awful feeling which your partner may be totally unconscious of and then you suddenly react fiercely. It is difficult to manage but it has got to be done positively on both sides.

'Sheila has displayed jealousy too. If she feels uncomfortable, I wouldn't let her stay that way and I certainly wouldn't say things like "Don't be stupid." It has got to be positive statements like, "I love you" or positive actions. If she thought I was looking at a woman at the next table, I would offer to change places.

'I feel I am a better person since Pam's time, although I do regret that marriage. I wish there had been a better way of learning – it was a hell of a painful way, for her too. I don't think in terms of whether I am happy. I think, "Where are we? Are we doing what we want to do?" I think in terms of okayness.

'Success is still important to me but having a home and a family are just pieces of a whole picture now, not the basis into which it all fits. I have a six-year-old son. He doesn't replace my other children, but it's a different world now. He is not part of my old scheme – two children and a house – he is his own person and I don't feel I have to parade him as mine.

'After thirteen years, my marriage is still fresh. I look forward to seeing Sheila – though perhaps not every night! Our sex life is good and we are still experimenting. I do feel this one is for life. But, if it did end, it wouldn't be as bad as the first time. I know who I am now. I'm not so frightened of being left hurt and alone.'

Pete doesn't present himself as a shining example of how swift remarriage can work. Many of his and Sheila's friends have divorced and he feels, in the light of what he has learned from them, that he was very lucky his second marriage worked.

'So many divorced men rush into any marriage just to get structure back into their lives. But when we talk to divorced friends, both Sheila and I say forget the structure, do a little exploration and live your life your own way. It is so important not to replace someone for the sake of it.

'In fact I think it is healthy perhaps not to have serious relationships till a year or two after a break-up. So Sheila and I were just very very lucky indeed.'

According to the National Marriage Guidance Council, second marriages are much more likely to work if both partners have come to terms with the failure of the first and have been able to learn positively from them, so as not to repeat the same mistakes. Blaming the other party and protesting innocence may aid the ego but is unlikely to bring any valuable self-knowledge. Whereas an ability to acknowledge one's own shortcomings and work on them may enable a suitable second marriage to iron out some of the insecurities which surfaced in the first.

Scriptwriter Morris thanks his second wife Jean, and the psychotherapy she encouraged him to embark on, for stopping what he foresaw as a cycle of interminable repeat performances. Droll and self-deprecating to the last, he views his past behaviour as acts of an arrested adolescent, totally incapable of seeing himself in the wrong. He, like Pete, suffered the extremes of jealousy. It was he who, he says, used his first wife Alice's early admission of an affair as a stick to beat her with ever afterwards. Both went along with the open marriage ethos of those times, however personally uncomfortable that may have made them, but while Morris always protested hurt and pain at Alice's extra-marital activities, he was inevitably surprised if she expressed hurt at his own.

Some months after the marriage ended he met a woman, also divorced with a child, and became involved with her for the next five years, although they didn't live together. 'I was looking for permanence at the start,' he said. 'I was looking to regain the smug contentment I had had during the best part of my marriage and I was looking for reassurance that I was still attractive and sexually adequate. I wanted conventional coupledom over again, everything on my terms.

'The relationship began with high romantic passion which levelled off, as it does. But one of the things I could never cope with was the dying down of passion. I felt it meant she didn't want me anymore. I was neurotically suspicious of every man in her life, including the postman. She tried to reassure me till she saw it didn't work and then we would row about it instead and I would twist all her words. There was nothing she could have done to convince me I was wrong, whatever she had tried.'

Four years into the relationship he moved back into his old family home, to be with his son Paul, then sixteen, when Alice moved to the country with her lover. It was only after that that he could get Alice to agree to a divorce. His relationship with his woman friend continued in a desultory way, although the possibility of marriage had been discussed and he had even been vasectomised with that in mind. Two years later, his son, with whom he had had a very close and rewarding relationship, went to work abroad.

'I went home, after seeing him off, feeling haunted and empty. My son would now just be a visitor in my life. I saw old age yawning ahead. There I was, freshly divorced and vasectomised and my son had left. I went into a depth of self-pity I had never managed before. I really did exceed myself. It must have been increasingly tiresome for my ladyfriend.

'She suggested we had some space apart, which in fact became permanent as she met someone else. At the same time, my ex-wife wanted me to sell our house because she needed her share of the money. So I foresaw myself with no home, no son and no woman. I felt my ladyfriend had "left" me, forgetting my role in that completely.

'It was a miserable winter but lessened by the advent of another lady, Jean. She was a widow and I had known her for some years. She came to stay as a guest in my house while waiting to buy one of her own, was very supportive and kind, and one thing led to another. We decided it would be sensible to buy a house together.

'I was still swanning around feeling self-pity and tormenting my previous woman with guilt. I would say to her, "If you ever start another relationship and it ends, I hope it isn't when your son has just left and your work is collapsing" etc, etc. I assumed none of the guilt at all.'

During that period, he and Jean found and bought a house. 'Very shortly I was into the euphoria of a new romance with her. I was forty-eight and behaving like a teenager. Jean doctored my wounds but refused to play my romantic love games. She didn't want affairs but she did want the freedom to live her life and carry on seeing her friends of either sex. She trusted me and wanted me to trust her. I, of course, expected to see my old female friends, but blew up if she saw men.

'Jean is very wise. She saw I had problems. As I continued to be unable to accept that she didn't feel euphoric teenage love, she started backing off and then I felt more and more panicky.

'One afternoon, I was walking down a street in town and saw her walking along with another man. She looked at me. I probably turned pale. My knees gave and I nearly fell. She said afterwards that she had tried to smile but it was difficult because I looked so stricken. I fell apart after that. I went home and crawled into a hole of depression and misery. When she came back we had a long talk. She reiterated that she had every right to walk down the street with a man she knew and that I had no right to assume that she had done anything more. But I felt it was all Jean's fault that she was with a man, even though I walk down streets with women I work with. Jean had indeed become uncomfortable about seeing any of her friends, because of my jealousy, but when she realised what my jealously was doing to her life, she put her foot down.

'Because I felt more for Jean than just teenage passion, a faint glimmer occurred to me that I might possibly be in the wrong. That was when she handed me, at just the right time, some simple psychology books which revealed to me all my ghastly manipulations and game-playing.'

He went to psychotherapy sessions for the next two years, a painful but very positive experience for him. He and Jean started getting on very well and have since married.

'I have started accepting things which previously would have thrown me into terror. I am very monogamous now and wouldn't even notice another woman. I also know, for the first time in my life, that I could handle solitude if necessary. It was Jean who pointed out that I had never been alone, there has hardly ever been a gap between relationships. I see so much in a different light. If only I had discovered earlier.

'I never wanted any relationship to stop being high romance. If it settled into contentment and affection, I would say, "Where's the romance gone? There must be another man!" I have had to accept that I'm so often taken over by the manipulative, spoilt child in me. Now that I have acknowledged that and got it out in the open, I hope that child has lost a lot of its power. I sometimes feel a stir of the old reflex. But I see myself doing it and can smile.'

Morris puts his changed persona down to luck – luck that he met someone perceptive enough not to go along with his unconscious game-playing and sensitive enough to coax him to take a longer look at himself at a time when he could respond. Dan also puts his present happiness down to luck. He could have embarked on a third disaster very easily, with two failed marriages already behind him and still no insight into how to meet his own needs. He seemed to have become accepting or resigned to personal tragedy in his life, although no more buffered against it.

It was he whose mother had rejected him when a child, farming him out to relatives and refusing to allow him to eat at the same table as his sister and herself when he was at home. He married for the first time very young. Both he and his wife were from poor backgrounds where the energy was expended on survival and the cold realities of life, and warmth and affection were alien to them both. The marriage collapsed when Dan did meet someone who could offer him warmth for the first time in his life. She died shortly before his divorce was finalised with bitterness on his ex-wife's part who for some time prevented him seeing his son.

He married again quite quickly after, to a woman whom, it emerged, was an alcoholic. Unable to help her, he spent most of his time caring for their son while she went off drinking, finally going for good. He fought for and won custody of their young son but his wife disappeared with him abroad and Dan has not seen him again. He went into clinical depression. 'It is a terrible thing when you don't know where in the world your child is. If there is a plane crash anywhere, you fear he is on it,' he said.

He met his present wife, whom he has been with for eighteen years, when she came to work for him as a secretary for the small business he had set up at his home. 'It was she who decided I was right for her,' he said. 'She once told me she wanted to marry me right from the start. I said, "Why? I was a mess," and she said she knew for sure when I lent her my new car, which I had never driven, to take her mother to hospital. The car came back with a big scratch and apparently I didn't complain, I just put it in for repair!'

He didn't have any qualms about marrying again. 'I have never felt I couldn't trust women. I have met far more untrustworthy men. And this marriage has been the pay-off for all that went before.

'I was forty-five and my wife was twenty-four. I have learned now what makes a good marriage for me, I didn't know before. We are very happy, it hasn't been hard work and I haven't had to change my character. She has made me so secure in myself that I don't *need* loving in the desperate way I used to. I just love having it!

'I used to think I must be the biggest fool on earth. But I have learned now that how I behaved in my life isn't as wrong as circumstances made me feel. I was stupid often, but stupid for fairly good reasons – lovingness rather than meanness.'

For the first time, he has been able to be a full-time father. 'It is smashing to grow up with my children this time and, because I am older, I am more relaxed with them. My priorities are all different. I know it doesn't really matter a damn if they leave the lights on or scrape the paintwork.

'I feel so secure now that I don't think I would even be that jealous if my wife, who is, after all, much younger than me, slept with another man just for sex. We are so right for each other that I see that as comparatively unimportant. I think sex and love get very confused. I was always attracted to women by their looks and, if you have an inclination for falling in love, like I did, you rationalise the rest of it. You learn later that being in love and loving someone are very different things.

'Young people tend to say "I love you" when they really mean "I lust." I say to my daughters, you might make love for fifteen hours a week but what are you going to do with the other 150 odd? Companionship and liking is the biggest thing.'

Both Morris and Dan have adjusted their ideas about the part passion plays in a marriage. Neither see it as unimportant, just less all-embracing. An American study of why marriages survive found that few couples still happily married long-term cited good sex as the reason for their marriages staying together. Most were still satisfied sexually, many said the passion had remained alive but a number said they were happy even though they had a less than ideal sexlife. It was largely agreed by the couples concerned that they would rather be married to their present partner and have a less than perfect sex life than be married to someone else with whom sex was better. And none saw affairs on the side as a compromise that worked.

For Ben, now married to Liz, sexual fidelity and personal security are a far more fulfilling exchange for the sexual freedom in affairs and the ensuing sexual and emotional insecurity he experienced in his 'open' marriage to Gail. He had found himself playing out a role that he had thought he ought to be 'adult' enough to accept. He thought he approved of Gail's boldness in having the courage to say she wanted to explore her sexuality further (she had been a virgin when she married Ben) and also thought initially he was comfortable following suit. But he found himself seeking sexual reassurance in his own liaisons, because he felt sexually challenged and made insecure by Gail's need to find her fuller satisfaction elsewhere.

He is also aware now that he was very self-obsessed in the early days of his marriage, struggling to find out who he really was and trying to make a success of his career. 'I can hardly even remember anything about our early marriage itself,' he admits. Gail may well have felt unfulfilled by their relationship. It was after her mother's death, which affected her profoundly, that she became seriously involved in affairs.

For Ben, after separation, it felt safer to settle for superficial sexual satisfaction than to risk the hurts from anything deeper. After years of avoiding acrimonious confrontation with Gail, his own hurts and needs were deeply suppressed. But he also knew that it was a lifestyle he did not find comfortable. Then he met Liz.

'Liz was very special because of her openness. She was open in a genuine way, with a lot of people in her life, whereas I was so repressed. That was what attracted me first,' he said. 'We built up very slowly. I didn't want to live with her initially became I had become very wary myself, after the marriage. But gradually things intensified. We shared so much more. I felt fully occupied by work and by Liz and was able to make the conscious decision that I didn't want other women.

'We were still living apart but the difficulty of "your place or my place" built up. It got to the point where it seemed ridiculous and destabilising to be apart – "I can't stay with you, I need to wear my pink tie tomorrow and that's at my place" syndrome.

'It was Liz who felt it more. She would say, you don't want a woman, you just want to live on your own and work. This was a new experience for me – someone feeling threatened by *my* behaviour. I had to let go of something in myself which tried to control things and decided to go along with whatever. I learned to trust my feelings without analysing a situation to death, and rationalising it. So we ended up living together and marrying.

'I don't have any idea of what fulfilment means so I can only make comparisons with my marriage to Gail. By comparison, this is fulfilling because there is much more of a feeling of learning and growing. There is a particular emotional flavour that makes it more of a full spectrum. The marriage to Gail was about escape from my parents, whereas the boundaries with Liz are much wider.

'The sharing of ideas is more truly compatible. And we do have rows and fights which clear the air. I have learned that rows can be functional instead of destructive.'

Dave also feels that a mixture of intimacy and personal space is what makes his second marriage with Julie a happy one. They share a great deal but also maintain a respect for each other as separate individuals. His long marriage to Anthea had been unhappy for many years. He had, he admits, lost interest in her once it was clear that they had little in common except the children. His had been a downhill path of heavy drinking and one-night stands until he finally walked out abruptly on his marriage. He stayed on sofas for several months before he had the money to rent a flat. He met Julie through work and, a year later, they bought a flat together.

'She is such a different person,' he enthuses. 'I enjoy her company immensely and we talk about everything, whereas Anthea and I found we could talk about nothing. After three years of marriage, Julie and I will still sit down together with a bottle of wine and just talk away the whole evening. We have separate evenings with our separate friends too. We respect each other's individuality, which was missing in my last marriage.

'I gave Anthea a lot of hurt, although, in the state I was in, I was past caring, I'm afraid. But I also now think that she didn't respect me either. She wanted me to act in certain ways. She didn't like it if I took an evening class or saw a male friend and I think she would have liked me to have a different job. She didn't support or have any interest in my work. I don't think either of us would have married each other if we had been older.' Anthea is also happily remarried.

He and Julie have a baby and he is thrilled to be a father again, although his other children have all grown up. 'Now I am mature and forty, I fully appreciate what children are about. I always did help with children and housework but this time I appreciate that Julie is bored being housebound and we will probably get a child-minder, so that she can work. Anthea too had felt bored but I never took her feelings seriously enough, probably because my father never let my mother work and that was where my ideas of marriage came from.'

Like Morris, he is making the effort to come to terms with insecurities about his wife's past lovers who have become friends. 'I remember going out with Julie and an ex of hers once and I did feel threatened, only to discover that he was feeling far more threatened and jealous of me. I can handle it now, men in Julie's past who are still friends. She sees nothing wrong with seeing a male friend alone and I trust her if she does.

'Once, I could never understand why Julie didn't feel jealous when I saw Anthea alone. But that is just not her way of thinking.'

Philip considers he was lucky to have found a partner who also is not easily sexually threatened as, in his case, his mistrust was of himself. His uncertainty about his own ability to be faithful was nearly sufficient to prevent him from embarking on what has been a very happy and fulfilling second marriage.

He had had no sexual experience when he first married in his early twenties. There was closeness and companionship between him and his wife but she, he felt, was not interested in the sexual side of their marriage. Spontaneous sexual attraction had not been a component of the attraction on either's part and Philip remained confused about his sexuality, frustrated and unfulfilled until, a few years into his marriage, he met a woman to whom he was overwhelmingly attracted. The dilemma he was caught in felt dire: affection, respect and responsibility towards his wife (and daughter) warring with a desperate need to fulfil his repressed basic sexual and emotional needs. He sought help from a psychiatrist who told him that he would have to have the affair or else have it forever in his head and that his marriage might or might not survive. It didn't and neither did the affair.

'I know the girl I had met was right for me,' he said. 'But neither of us could square what had happened with our consciences. By that time I had divorce proceedings pending, I was deeply troubled by not being allowed proper access to my child and, for her part, she couldn't take the disapproval and pressure from her parents. Sadly we ended by having a stormy parting.'

The tragedy's profound effects included an unconquerable confusion about his sexual and emotional needs, and a fear that he would never be able to assuage them all in one place.

'I felt that my relationships were doomed to failure and my lack of confidence probably contributed to their failure. I met my present wife Karen three years after my divorce. She became a very special person for me but I still had to have other affairs, which we managed to weather.

'When we did marry, two years ago, I was still worried that I might find I needed other relationships. I had discovered my sexuality so late and I have always craved warmth and physical contact. I didn't get enough of it as a child and sometimes I feel I may never get enough, I seem to need so much.

'Karen and I took the step to marry, despite my worries, because we had known each other a few years by then and the relationship couldn't go any further until it was on a different footing. Karen would have been happy enough just to live with me but I suggested marriage because I knew that was really what she wanted, and she mattered enough to me.

'She has had a lot of time to get to know me and the intuition to see beyond what I wouldn't see or speak of. If, in the next eighteen months, I did have an affair, I think we could survive it. I haven't had affairs. My fear has been merely that I would want to. As it is, our relationship grows and builds every day.

'In the early days, I did find myself attracted to another woman but I stopped myself from pushing anything further because I could see nothing good could come of it. It wouldn't help the woman or Karen or make me happy either. I don't even find it easy to cope with more than one relationship at once anyway.

'I think the idea of an affair seems to offer me the physical warmth and comfort I crave without the complicated emotions that go with adult relationships. I find myself looking for what I missed as a child and that is impossible, because affairs develop and grow too.

'Karen has been a terrific support to me as well as a marvellous companion. I am getting happier all the time and I'm more at one with my make-up. Fortunately my sexual pre-occupation is finally dwindling.'

Not all the second marriages have been so successful as those described so far. A couple of men, Jay and Laurie, agree that they rushed into second marriage, perhaps unwittingly set on securing a substitute and with no self-knowledge gained from the first to sustain it. In a few other cases, the complex problems of feeling caught between the emotional needs of children of the previous marriage and second wife caused considerable pain and sometimes led to separation. The men all specified their regret that, in any conflict, they had tended to side with the children, through guilt, or had ignored it which did not help either their own or their children's relationship with the stepmother.

Joe was bringing up his children alone, after his wife left him for another man, when he started to see a woman he had met through work. 'Susan started coming round and helping me a lot and the children seemed to like her,' he said. 'I didn't want her to live there until I was sure – I didn't even want the children to know if she stayed the night. Things were fine when she finally moved in but then she started pressuring me into marrying her. I knew it felt wrong and yet, in the end, I did. As soon as we were married, she started pressuring for a child. It was "I'm looking after your two, I want one of my own" sort of stuff. We had a child within a year and that was when my second wave of problems started.

'Susan felt that our child was more special than mine and my children's fondness for her started to fade. Even outsiders noticed her favouritism. She wasn't nasty, she just wasn't interested in my two. I found myself trying to please everybody, and trying to give my kids extra attention. It didn't work and no one was pleased.

'Then my two said, "We think we would like to live with mummy." That really choked me but I didn't want them to suffer, so I said okay. They then started coming to our house every other Sunday and Susan was okay about that, because they weren't living with us anymore. But I found myself becoming more and more resentful towards Susan because I knew it was her attitude that had led to their leaving. I loved those kids and because I had brought them up, I felt even closer to them than normal.'

Joe's bitterness about Susan's attitude towards his children led to the start of rows. Communication dwindled, although both he and she adored their daughter. 'Susan started going out a lot, as we weren't on great terms. Then the phone calls with no one at the other end started coming, but this was the second time round for me and I was wise to that sort of thing now.

I finally got it out of her that there was someone else in her life. I was actually pleased by that time. I invited her bloke round and told them both to go.

'Susan said she was taking our daughter and that broke my heart. She was even more devoted to me than the other two were and was very upset. Susan married again after our divorce and has three more children but my daughter would prefer to live with me because she doesn't like the husband. We had a chat and I tried to explain that life isn't always rosy. She is too young to live with me because now, in my job, I leave the house too early and get home too late. I told her she could ring me or stay the night any time she wants. It seems to have gone down reasonably well. She does ring me but there are no requests to stay the night.'

Joe now has a girlfriend but he doesn't plan to marry again, even though she gets on well with his daughter and he doesn't fear a repeat of the recent past. 'I know I won't marry. I can't see the point if there aren't to be kids and I don't want any more now. She knows that. I think she would like the security of marriage but marriage isn't much security these days.' He has a very close relationship with all his children, the elder two of whom are grown up.

'My daughter's happy and my son and I are just like buddies. We go on holidays, go to football. He is very anti-marriage, however. I feel that's a shame. Every relationship is different. It's what you make it.'

Joe was already in his second marriage and the father of a further child when the friction between new wife and the children of the last marriage started. Many men may have an earlier warning of dissension because their children react badly from the start to someone they see as a supposed replacement for their mother. Careful counselling may help, if their fears are psychological rather than personal, but if the dislike on either side is strong, then it comes down to a very difficult choice: whom to put first, the wife-to-be or the children? According to one marriage guidance expert, that has to be a very personal decision, and, however painful, better made positively, confronting all the guilt or resentment in advance.

Robert, the builder, had the decision to make twice. The first time he avoided it. The second time unfortunately he chose too late to save his second marriage. His personal story is a tragic one.

After his wife had left him for other men, he looked after their daughter Mandy until he found himself physically and emotionally unable to cope. Reluctantly he decided Mandy would be better off with her mother who at least had a family network to help her cope. He was twenty-four.

He himself went to lick his wounds at his sister's home, 150 miles away.

He remained withdrawn and unhappy for several months until his nephews, then teenagers, persuaded him to go out to clubs. Then he started to drink heavily to drown his sorrows.

'I moved into a bedsitter. I didn't have any relationships with women because I was so resentful and bitter towards them all. I was twenty-four and an old man.' When, eventually, emboldened by drink, he did embark on one-night stands, 'I treated women like doormats because of the chip on my shoulder.' It was a year before he could trust sufficiently to form a relationship, with a woman herself in the process of divorce. He was ready to marry her and take on her two children when he was devastated, yet again, by her decision to return to her husband whom, he found out, she had been seeing all along.

'If I thought I was bitter before, this time was worse. I really dived into heavy drinking and practically became an alcoholic. When I met my second wife Maureen, I didn't intend anything to get serious. I carried on drinking and seeing other women. I had built up a barrier around myself and wouldn't let anyone inside. I had a couldn't-care-less attitude. I was Jack the lad, always joking and laughing and drinking, money no object. I think that was what attracted Maureen. She was only eighteen, lived with her parents and was a typist in a local firm. I introduced her to a completely different lifestyle. But I had no consideration for her feelings. One night I had invited her round, then another woman turned up and I ordered Maureen out. I thought, if anyone had feelings for me, it was their hard luck.

'For a few years I just fitted her in when I had the time. I had no idea until much later how unhappy she had felt. She decided she had had enough and stopped seeing me, and then suddenly the boot was on the other foot. I realised she really loved me and I had lost something very good.

'I won her over and we got a flat together. Then I started getting calls from my ex-wife. She had been disabled in a car accident and couldn't cope with Mandy. It was a dreadful shock to learn what had happened to her. So Mandy came to live with me. She was very upset about leaving her mother and she had already had a turbulent childhood. By that time she was twelve. Both she and Maureen were competing for my attention and I felt more responsible to Mandy so their relationship was very stormy. Maureen was only a youngster herself. She couldn't handle it and went back to her parents.

'It was like another body blow. I gave up work to look after Mandy and had very mixed feelings. I was the father of a girl who had been through a hell of a lot and I had doubts about whether I could give her proper care and attention. For the previous several years I had lived as a single man and it was hard being a full-time parent again.

'Then Maureen decided to come back. I got a special licence and within a week we were married. But Mandy became a dreadful handful. She felt that Maureen resented her deeply. She started stealing from her purse and being very rude. But when Maureen complained, I still defended Mandy. Then Mandy started glue-sniffing and it all got too much. Maureen finally said, "It's Mandy or me" and this time I chose Maureen.

'Mandy wanted to go back to her mother anyway but, in the end, because her mother couldn't cope, she ended up being fostered. I felt so terrible about that. But I also felt I had to try to save my marriage and that she would in the end be better with foster parents who had children. She would have a stability I felt incapable of giving her.'

Robert didn't manage to save his marriage. By trying, out of a sense of guilt and responsibility, to take Mandy's part against Maureen, he ended up compounding his problems. Maureen felt resentful towards Robert for not standing up for her while Robert found he felt resentful about her rejection of Mandy. Gradually they began to drift apart.

'She told me that I was boring and dull. She had fallen in love with the "Jack the lad" that wasn't really me at all. My true side is my home-loving side – I had always felt the want of a solid homelife after my own lack of one as a child. She also told me how hurt she had been by my behaviour towards her before we were married and that she wants to get her own back on men now,' he said. Sadly, his own history of hurt is now repeating itself in her, while he feels not bitter, this time, but numbed. Their separation is very recent.

For Frank there has been a happier ending to the ructions that occurred when he started living with Penelope, his second wife-to-be. His children were living with Sarah but visiting him every other weekend. Penelope moved in six months after Frank and Sarah had split.

'It was very difficult at first. The children probably thought she was the reason for my leaving. They resented her but she was very good about them and tried to forge her own relationship with them. Six months later, the situation reached a head. Much of it was my fault. I let the children do what they wanted, because of my guilt, instead of disciplining them. They would fight for my attention and were adept at manipulating any situation in order to get it. Children are. So Penelope started to feel resentful and I was glossing things over and trying to keep them smooth.

'We all ended up having a real screaming match one weekend. I told Penelope to say exactly what she felt, even though they were my children.

It was frightening what came out. Afterwards, the children didn't want to come again. I felt terrible and Penelope felt very torn because, although she didn't want the problem, she was very sad for me.

'I now understand it was a predictable pattern. If we had known, we might have been better able to cope. My daughter started visiting again, my son wouldn't. It was then we decided on family therapy and I also carried on with personal therapy of my own.

'The relationship between Penelope and the children, and myself and the children, is much better now. Both came to our wedding. But I don't see that I can do an awful lot to help them more until I have sorted myself out psychologically. I feel I have hurt them so much.

'As a child, I was never encouraged to express anger or tears or to talk about my feelings. Sarah and I didn't discuss anything but Penelope and I discuss everything now. I have learned one hell of a lot, though it was very upsetting to have to go through that one real screaming match to learn.

'I try to encourage my children to express their feelings, however negative. I don't think they should be shielded from problems. It doesn't help in the end.

'In a way I hope that Sarah doesn't remarry. Her husband would probably have gone through what we went through. I suspect it may be necessary or inevitable,' he said.

Stuart, however, has not found that the case. He was the only man I spoke to who became a stepfather. His second wife Margaret has two sons. 'Because of the person she is,' he says, 'it was very easy to take them on. She is prepared to share them. We both tell them off, when necessary. They were twelve and fourteen when I came into their lives and they seemed to accept me.

'Sometimes there were some problems when they had spent the weekend with their father and then came back to us but, in general, it was a very cosy transfer. I don't try to take the place of their father but, in some ways, Margaret says she feels that I am more of a father to them than their own. I think we just both have our own relationships with them and they seem to appreciate each of us in different ways.'

Stuart describes his marriage to Margaret as enormously happy. After his first wife Celia left him, he was conscious of feeling some trepidation about the idea of serious involvements. 'I felt, "I'm single, I'm going to do what I want to do, and I'll never marry again." I had a fear of getting too deep into a relationship that I couldn't get out of. I had three or four affairs and then, a year later, met Margaret and had no wish at all to get out!' he said. 'It became serious very quickly and the feeling was marvellous.

'At first I was over-anxious for it to work. I started looking out for anything that was going wrong so that we could correct it at once. But now I'm relaxed. There just isn't that sort of need. We lived together for a couple of years and when we married it was because we wanted to marry, not because of any external pressure or practicalities.

'Love, for me, is a feeling of contentment, of wanting all you possibly can for the other person and completely sharing everything. Margaret and I discuss everything and do everything together. We just don't feel the need for any freedom from each other, or to spend an evening apart. That happens to be us, and the way we like things.'

They are partners in every sense of the word, as Stuart gave up his company job to set up a shop with Margaret, selling musical instruments. They are with each other virtually twenty-four hours a day and yet Stuart feels freer than he ever did before. 'Margaret's support and enthusiasm has given me the push I needed to take risks and make changes. I feel anything's possible. If an interesting opportunity came up for me somewhere else, she would say, "Go on. Let's do it!" I used to spend too much time holding myself back and thinking I was doing it for the sake of my first wife.'

He regrets what he now sees as wasted years spent in his first marriage, with neither he nor his first wife able to give each other happiness as he knows it now. But he also acknowledges what others who are now happily re-married acknowledge: that without what was so painfully learned first time round, they would not have made the self-discoveries and changes that gave them a second chance to find happiness in marriage.

# Reflections

Whenever I mentioned that I was writing a book about divorced men, people tended to ask what I had found to be the common themes. I was far more aware, however, of how different each man's experience and responses were from the next, and how the range of their feelings were as likely to be similar to those of women I know as to those of men. I do think men and women are very different beings but that certain feelings are fundamental to us all and have their main differences in expression.

After I had completed the interviews for this book, I had a long conversation with Renate Olins, director of the London Marriage Guidance Council and asked her what major differences she had found in men and women's attitudes and reactions to difficulties in relationships. There was only one generalisation that she felt comfortable about making.

'Men, on the whole, do seem to find it less acceptable than women to express their feelings, and particularly difficult to acknowledge those to do with weakness and vulnerability,' she said. 'They are often less good at putting what is wrong into words but they feel it all just the same.'

It is a difference which perhaps isn't news to any of us. What is more surprising is that it all seems to come down to that one. Most of us have been brought up to believe that man is strong and woman is weaker, emotionally as well as physically. And while the women's movement has done much to confound the expectation that women should be weak, it has been far more difficult for men to draw back from the expectation that they should be strong, as it is always harder to move from a position of perceived strength to one of perceived weakness. Perception is perhaps the crucial word because we all have vulnerabilities, whether or not we show them. But the effects of concealing them, especially from ourselves, can, as we have seen, be crippling.

In the realm of developmental psychology, there is plenty of material to draw from to explain why we collectively, if unconsciously, have different expectations of the characters of boys and girls. Also some psychologists concerned with the physical functioning of the brain say that there are inherent differences in the brains of men and women which may then be further enhanced by social learning. It is difficult ever to be sure where one process starts and the other stops.

But let us start with the findings from biology. It is a contentious field but, as researchers are always quick to point out, their findings refer to those elusive beings, the average male and the average female, and not to individuals of either sex who of course will vary from each other.

The main discovery has been that differences between the sexes, in personality, skills and interests may be due to the different ways that male and female brains are organised and develop. The part of the brain that governs, amongst other things, verbal skills develops earlier in females and superiority in those skills is retained. The same is true of males and spatial skills which involve seeing. Different combinations of skills are also more prevalent in one sex or the other because of how and where these are centred in male or female brains.

In the 1970s, interest in the role of sex differences in the brain spawned a mass of research, much of which was decried as not sufficiently scientific. Two well-respected neuro-psychologists, Diane McGuinness and Karl Pribram, sifted through it all and attempted to summarise what they considered the valid findings of a brain-based difference in the abilities of men and women.

The part of their summary that is relevant here is that men's skills in perception of depth and space make them better at mechanical tasks and more interested in objects than people. They have a curiosity which leads them to be distracted more easily, and they are more interested in exploring new territory than consolidating old. Women excel in verbal skills and tasks that require fine coordination. They have better hearing and are more sensitive to touch. They are more interested in people, more attentive to sounds and their emotional meaning, and more socially responsive and empathetic.

In conclusion, McGuinness and Pribram define man as a 'manipulative animal', expressing himself in actions, while woman is more of a 'communicative animal, preferring to transmit and receive.'

What does it all mean in terms of relationships between men and women? As the researchers have themselves said, none of their findings mean that men and women are precluded from sharing each other's special skills or even excelling in them but that their natural abilities are strongest in the areas indicated. And here social learning comes in. Perhaps because boys are still treated so differently from girls, at home and/or at school, and because their natural instinct is to be interested in things outside rather than inside themselves, they have less opportunity to develop their emotional life and less awareness that something is missing.

Certainly a number of the men I spoke to recalled seeing their own childhood family life as the model on which all family life is based. 'I didn't know it could be different', they said, when talking of home lives where little emotion was expressed. It could be that boys are on the whole less aware of others' inner worlds, whereas for girls these are subjects of intense discussion.

That we compound any differences in the rates at which male and female abilities develop is evident from much research into the treatment by parents and teachers of boys and girls. Dr Robert Ornstein has summarised the research work in his book *Psychology: The Study of Human Experience*. First, he makes the point that, from day one, there are significant differences in the way that parents respond to opposite sex babies.

Both parents, but particularly fathers, are likely to describe their newborn daughters as soft, small, delicate and weak and their newborn sons as strong, firm and hardy, whatever they in fact look like. When the babies cry, parents more usually attribute that to anger in a boy and fear in a girl. (Yet in experiments where adults have been deceived as to the babies' sex, the girls togged out in blue and the boys in pink, they have attributed those sort of characteristics and responses quite happily to the wrong sex baby.)

As Ornstein points out, from studies, girls and boys at the age of one do not have preferences for playing with dolls rather than lorries or vice versa. But if parents make sex-based judgements in terms of the toys they give their children, which they usually do, the children develop a clear preference in that direction by the time they are three.

Little boys are tossed about and swung more, in play with their parents, whereas little girls are kept closer to the mother's side. It seems, however, that fathers are consistently more responsible for sex-based distinctions made between boy and girl children than women are. They encourage rough and tumble play in boys and, according to one study, often show disapproval if a son likes to play with girls.

As boys get older, they are encouraged by fathers to act very differently from girls. As Ornstein summarises the findings, 'Boys are likely to be encouraged to compete and achieve, to be independent and responsible, and to control their feelings.' Father are stricter with sons, punishing them more when they don't meet standards set, whereas girls are more likely to be trusted, although they are supervised more, and more likely to receive more physical warmth from both parents. At school, teachers tend to follow suit.

Whatever the variations on the theme, and however enlightened individual parents and teachers want to be, much is the same today as before such differences were ever questioned. But, whereas the socio-economic climate is such that girls are now less likely to suppress their intellects and initiative, it is far harder to unlearn the emotional suppression, which boys may not even be aware of.

When we are children, we all learn our ideas about what it is right or wrong to be and how to behave from the reactions of our parents. We look for clues and pick up on cues, however small, such as a nod, an expression of interest or a puckered lip. Males tend to learn that expression of feelings such as fear or insecurity or desire for affection do not bring acceptance and encouragement from their parents. They may grow up believing that only if they are strong and fearless or intellectual giants will they warrant and receive the love and affection they need – conditional love which humanistic psychologist Carl Rogers was one of the first to point to as the cause of much identity confusion in adult life.

I recall the man who said to me so plaintively that he craved so much physical affection he feared he could never get enough of it. He had been very deprived of it as a child, although his intellectual abilities had been well and lovingly nourished. It isn't only males, of course, who may have childhoods deprived of enough warmth and affection. But males, on the whole, may be less able to identify that lack at the time perhaps because, as the brain research indicated, their energies are outward- rather than inward-directed. I recall, too, the man who said to me that perhaps the only way to relinquish the hold of unmet emotional needs from childhood is to pit oneself against the elements and canoe down the rapids. There they do not matter. The battle is with elements *outside* of oneself.

I was interested by the fact that so many of the men I spoke to spontaneously mentioned their parents and their upbringing when talking of how they came to marry and how they behaved within their marriages. As men whose marriages had gone wrong, they had had much time to reflect on what they could see as the whys and wherefores of it all. But at least two of the men who feel they understand themselves better now said they had rushed into second marriages without reflecting on why the first failed, and only took a deeper look, through therapy, after the shock of a second failure as well. It is always far from easy to make the connections between what we were brought up to expect and how we behave.

The elements of our experience we end up bringing with us vary enormously. Some of the men I spoke to had become imbued, unconsciously, with the mores learned at home, to be strong, dependable and dutiful. Others had identified aspects of their homelife that they didn't like and determined to be different, such as the man who felt it important to 'bust away' from his family and then found it difficult to cope when his wife was very family-minded; or the man who saw his own parents' marriage as boring and stultifying and wanted something different, yet found himself unconsciously conditioned as to 'right' and 'wrong' ways to behave and repeating what he saw as the same mistakes. Almost all learned to keep emotions hidden and concentrate on external things instead.

As Renate Olins says, 'We all bring luggage from the past into our marriages.' We want the same or we want something different from what we have known and when the chosen partner isn't in fact entirely the same or entirely different, we feel cheated. One couple shared a fear of acrimonious accusations and displays of anger because they had both seen and feared those outbursts of hostile emotion in their parents, both sets of whom divorced. They agreed to run their lives differently but had no way of coping with resentful feelings, that aroused the anger that they had agreed not to express, without hurting each other in other ways. Meanwhile those who said that they had come from stable homes, meaning those where any ripples of anxiety or anger did not reach the surface, found themselves ill-equipped to deal with a very different emotional climate in their own marriages.

These are not differences but similarities between the experience of men and women, but women may – just may be quicker on the whole to identify and perceive what is wrong. A number of men said to me, 'I didn't even know anything was wrong' or 'I didn't see it coming', even though, in retrospect, they know they were not happy. It was surprising too how a number of men commented on the lack of training about relationships at school, an acknowledgement of the fact that, as boys, their interests and concerns weren't remotely directed towards interaction or creating emotional harmony at home. I cannot imagine women making such a comment, not because they necessarily learnt any more but because their natural interests are usually more inclined that way.

Even if psychologists are right and women are more generally sensitive and empathetic about people, I think we do tend to play our part in promoting any emotional gap between men and women. Most women probably do want partners who are 'strong', in whatever terms they choose to interpret that word. Some still want the traditional cosseting and protection, others want someone who is at least as strong-minded or strong-willed as themselves, in whatever areas are deemed important, although this is probably of less concern to men than women. So inner strength and outer strength may still become confused. It takes inner strength to show one's vulnerability to someone but that show of vulnerability may be threatening to the other person if it is something they don't want to face, in their partner or in themselves, and that may send the barriers up again.

A couple of men mentioned being seen as father figures by their wives. One recalled the first time he had shown his weakness to his wife – in an incident too personal and painful for him to detail – and how he quickly realised that this was not acceptable to her, putting that side of himself away and carrying on performing his role as protector. His wife was by no means a traditionally-minded woman. She was effectively established in her own career. Another man recalled feeling expected to give comfort to his wife about her insecurities over the relationship without feeling able to express his own. He saw his role as being the responsible, strong one and willingly, if uncomfortably, entered into that collusion with his wife, until his inability to find the right solutions burst the bubble.

Men in their marriages are just as likely to be motivated by the same things that motivate women. Two men mentioned very desperately wanting their own home, and one saw himself as happiest when a homebody. Several attractive men were just as insecure about whether they could really be sure of being wanted and two were amazed to find that they could inspire love and passion – qualities the stereotypical male is supposed to take for granted. The need to be cared for as well as carers comes across in men's admission of resentment towards attention-demanding babies. But sometimes these feelings may be disguised in what are to them more acceptable forms.

One man recognised, for instance, that his jealousy and possessiveness about his wife was a camouflage not for insecurity about her love for him but for insecurity about himself, and what he wanted and was capable of achieving. Somewhere hidden in his mind he feared that he didn't have much to offer. Some avoided confronting the source of their own feelings of lack of fulfilment by seeing their wives' insecurity or over-dependence as the problem and trying to help them sort their personalities out without involving themselves in the equation. By trying to be 'helpful' and caring instead of voicing their own needs and wants, no truly useful communication could ensue and their own fears could remain unconfronted.

Also, for men more than women the expressions of emotion may be channelled into sex, which seems a more comfortable, if not necessarily always appropriate, repository for them. American psychotherapist Lillian B. Rubin, in her book *Intimate Strangers*, puts it down to the fact that men's first identification is with a woman, their mother, and that when they learn that they are different and must identify with men, they lose trust in their own emotional responses.

She says: 'For men, the repression of their first identification and the muting of emotional attachment that goes with it fit neatly with cultural proscriptions about manliness that require them to abjure the emotional side of life in favour of the rational. Sex, therefore, becomes the one arena where it is legitimate for men to contact their deeper feeling states and to express them. Indeed, all too often, the sex acts carries most of the burden of emotional expression for men – a reality of their lives that may explain the urgency with which men so often approach sex. For, if sex is the main conduit through which inhibited emotions are animated, expressed and experienced, then that imperative and compulsive quality that seems such a puzzle becomes understandable.'

It is an interesting theory and brings to mind for me many things that various men said. One became aware that he had been looking for relief from or resolution of quite unrelated worries through sex and it ceased to be satisfying because it was not through sex that he could resolve financial or work preoccupations that were making him insecure about himself. Another laughed at himself for presuming that if sex with his wife or, later, girlfriend of long standing, ceased to remain high passion, she must have found someone else. Sex needed, for him, to be ever a momentous emotional experience of exalted order.

Some men mentioned that, when seeking casual affairs after their marriage breakdown, they were unable to refrain from behaving in an emotionally intense fashion, even if they did not feel fully emotionally involved. In all these cases, it certainly seems that the sexual act carried much more than sex-related feelings. On the other side of the same coin, men are more likely, according to Renate Olins, to see their marital difficulties as stemming from unsatisfactory sex rather than emotional barriers which then manifest themselves in sex. Having channelled their emotional expression into sex, they may find it difficult to see that simple sex therapy is not really their solution. I am reminded also of the man I spoke to who said that he had had no idea that he wasn't communicating with his wife and thought, when he ceased to want sex with her, that he must be becoming homosexual.

The traditional view of men and women's approach to sex is that women must feel an emotional connection before they want a sexual connection whereas men may generate the former from the latter. In the current climate, it is certainly not true that women need to feel an emotional connection first. Very many feel perfectly happy to make or initiate purely sexual liaisons and are as wary as many men of any emotional commitment. The differences lie at a deeper level, according to one psychotherapist I spoke to.

'I feel women are just as capable as men of taking charge and going for excitement from sex, when it is on a superficial level,' she said. 'But when a deeper emotional commitment has been made between a man and woman, the quality of the sexual relationship changes. Sex is not the only way a woman expresses herself emotionally and she may want it less because, when she does, she is giving herself very deeply.'

If sex is seen as more central to men than to women, on the whole, marriage is seen as more central to women than to men. Some men, as did one or two I spoke to, see having a wife as part of the whole package of success that includes career, house, possessions and children. Women too might want the husband and the house and the family but they are less likely to think of all or any as part and parcel of their success or acceptance in their career. As one man put it, the wife and family may be a support system to men whereas for women, whether they work or not, the family and marriage usually remain central or certainly of equal import. It is more often men who go out from the marriage and do other things while women are more tied to the children. Even in cases where responsibilities are shared or *seen* by men as shared, final responsibility usually rests with the woman. One man said: 'I thought I was wonderful, bathing the baby, but it was never me who got up to him at night.' It usually isn't the man, either, who remembers when vaccinations are due or makes arrangements for the dentist, even if he may be the one to take the children along on the day.

Quite a large number of the ex-wives of the men I spoke to appeared not have worked during the marriage, while bringing up children. In some cases, their finances made that a matter of choice, but, in some others, the husband was the one who felt he should be the breadwinner. Whatever the circumstances, quite a number of the women, in the way that they were described by their husbands, appeared to be very dependent, emotionally and financially. It is not surprising, perhaps, that financial dependence should lead to emotional dependence but reducing the matter to economic cause and effect may actually be misleading.

I noticed, for instance, that it was a man whose partner was busy building up her own career when they met who said that, very shortly after, *he* became her life and her career ceased to mean anything. They did not have children. Nor did the man who was the one who mentioned, when talking of his wife, that women see marriage as central while for men it is a support system. Women are traditionally seen as dependent while men are independent and we resort to those words perhaps too readily when seeking explanations for behaviour. What is seen as dependency may in fact be a strong desire for connection and attachment, wanted by both sexes but more readily repressed by men for all the reasons mentioned earlier. The closer the woman moves, the more the man retreats, engendering in the woman insecurity which may well tip into dependence.

The man may retreat in socially acceptable ways. A number of men said that they worked all hours so that the fruits of their labours could benefit their families – nice homes, holidays abroad, sometimes private education for the children. I questioned whether they did not underestimate the degree to which their actions were dictated by their own needs to fulfil themselves outside the marriage. On reflection, they admitted that the need for personal fulfilment and success was a strong motivating force.

If that wasn't acknowledged or considered, perhaps there was no chance to look at any issues beneath. Possibly non-working wives felt ungrateful if they complained; or the necessity for the husband to work long hours was agreed by both, in collusion to avoid facing friction in the marriage or to dilute its impact. In becoming more and more 'dependent' a woman may lose her own real sense of personal autonomy and identity, and feel frustrated in all ways, while a man, by asserting his independence, can at least deny his deeper, uncomfortable dependency needs. It is interesting that, in surveys, divorced or widowed women are more likely to say they would not marry again, whereas most men say that they would.

We all have ambivalent needs for both dependence and independence and it takes considerable security to meet both. Yet the commitment of marriage doesn't necessarily provide that security, particularly if marriage is seen as a state rather than a continual process. As one man described marriage: 'Once you go into that comfort zone, playing house, you don't have to think about yourself so much. There's a sort of symbiosis that blocks real discovery of self.' And another: 'In order to live with someone, you step into role-playing and then you are no longer free to be who you are.' Social expectations of marriage can mask needs instead of fulfilling them.

I recall, for instance, the man who had felt smothered by what he saw as the emotional dependency of his wife yet, when after divorce he became involved with a woman much 'stronger' than himself, he experienced exactly the same needs for reassurance and attention that his wife had done. He had recognised his dependency need only when he met a woman who, like him, had denied her own. It is interesting that he described her as 'stronger' than himself, meaning perhaps that her emotional neediness was even more repressed that his own. And that takes me back to an earlier point, that we seem to confuse inner and outer strength and imagine that displays of neediness and vulnerability cannot go alongside of confidence or assertion or independence. As a result, we may fail to acknowledge and communicate all our needs.

Failure to communicate fully and directly was mentioned and stressed by so many men that I spoke to. While communication may not magic problems away, it does enable positions to become clearer and decisions to be faced about whether partners can or cannot fulfil each other's important needs. But it's so hard to dare to voice deep and hurtful negative feelings, fearful the relationship may not survive them and frightened to take the risk, unless it has already degenerated into mutual abuse. It feels less deeply threatening, although just as painful, sometimes just to go into an emotional freeze and close up completely. It is then that so many couples think of trial separations. The men I spoke to found those didn't work.

'Trial separations,' said Renate Olins, 'are only useful if the time is used by couples to learn about themselves. They are facing two equally painful alternatives – staying together or splitting up – and if these are blocked out of their minds while apart, the time won't have helped for understanding what has gone wrong. For a lot of people, it is just harder to return to each other after a break.'

If counselling hasn't been considered or tried before the crunch comes, where else is there to turn for support? For women, far more than for men in our culture, there are close, intimate friends.

It is a pattern that has become established by the early teens, and not only in our own culture, according to psychologists who have researched the role of friendship. At the age of four or five, however, it is boys who prefer to stay in very small groups, resenting intrusion from outside, while girls are more gregarious and bossy and like to draw other children into their circle. It is in early adolescence that the roles switch, boys preferring gangs and girls preferring intimate friendships with one or two best female friends.

The switch may well be linked to the apparently differing development of the male and female brain, with boys becoming ever more action-oriented and girls more communication-oriented. Boys are looking to test their independence and leadership abilities, take risks and explore outside themselves while girls become concerned with relationships and interpersonal skills. As adults, men may exchange the loose groups of which they were a part, as boys, for the casual network of work or pub acquaintances or sports partners.

The paucity of really intimate friendship between males, in general, is something Lillian Rubin has given much thought to in her book *Intimate Strangers*. She believes that, for men, emotional needs are more likely to be invested in one woman, whereas for women these needs are rarely invested exclusively in one man. She found, in a survey of over 200 men, that over two thirds of single men couldn't identify a best friend at all and, for those who could, it was likely to be a woman. The married men tended to name their wives as their one trusted confidante whereas the married women named their husbands and women friends.

Men who did claim to have close male friends tended to talk with them about shared activities rather than talking openly of themselves, their worries, or seeking emotional support. Any discussions about marital relationships tended to be abstract or jokey. Some told Dr Rubin that they couldn't risk showing themselves in a vulnerable light to other men; others claimed that marital difficulties were private and required loyalty and discretion. But, when questioned, it became clear that these men did not talk to other men about *anything* that made them vulnerable – worries about their position at work, for instance, even though no loyalty was required there.

I remember one man I spoke to had himself given quite a bit of thought to the fact that, when he separated from his wife, he found he had no friends. The 'friends' had been his wife's and, along with their husbands, spent evenings with them socially. I say 'friends' in quotation marks because the man had considered them and their husbands as such, although he only had a superficial social relationship with them – and hadn't then noted the fact. He found that he himself had only a loose circle of acquaintances from work and volunteered the view that men see each other as rivals, not confidants.

Rubin's suggested explanation for the difference is psychoanalytical and goes back to her Freudian stance that boys feel deeply rejected when they learn they have to detach themselves from identification with their mothers and assert themselves as members of an opposite sex, at that point alien to them.

A man as a boy, she says, 'had to renounce his earliest bond – a renunciation that meant also he lost touch with a part of himself, the part that can allow vulnerability, that can experience dependency. Forever after, therefore, he'll search for relationships which offer the promise of healing the wound, of regaining that lost part. But, because the original connection was with a woman, it's usually only with her that it can be re-experienced at all.' Safer unconsciously to deny the need, through fear of abandonment yet again, and establish social roles that aid the denial.

In her theory, then, males may cut themselves off from emotional closeness in any human quarter. But, whatever the reasoning, it is very plain that men on whole do not have the same intimate support systems of women and suffer more, physically, when their marriages collapse. Divorced men report much more ill-health than women, in terms of stress-related diseases. Emotions are turned inwards, instead of outwards, and take their toll on the body.

A number of the men I spoke to did claim that they had close friends to talk to, but most of the friends were women. In common with many other men, they said, 'I didn't feel a man would understand, if he weren't in the same position.' Those who did know men who were divorced tended to find a barrier had been broken down – they knew they both had shared an emotionally shattering experience. But I remember one man I spoke to emphasising the practical quality of that support – advice on what bedding etc. he would need to acquire for the children to use when they stayed at weekends – important stuff indeed, but interestingly the only example he gave me of the value of his having a friend.

Quite a few men did have to explore their painful, tangled feelings alone, after they broke up with their wives, and for some the process took a good couple of years before they regained a sense of their own worth. Their experience is not universal but it is undoubtedly common. The struggle must be an extra agonising one when the vocabulary of the inner emotional debate is so unfamiliar.

So it certainly made sense to me that those who had sought counselling at some stage felt so much more at ease with discussion of their emotions, and valued the experience as so important. Twice as many women as men seek help from Marriage Guidance Councils, although more and more couples now do attend together. According to Renate Olins, director of the London branch, men do, on whole, find it harder to start talking about their emotions, once there, and often try to keep the discussions on a practical level.

'A lot of men find it difficult to acknowledge feelings to do with weakness and vulnerability,' she said. 'They feel that if they use emotive words – like fear – they will lose control of the situation. But by acknowledgement, in fact, we can start to *gain* control because only when we have acknowledged a feeling can we begin to deal with it.'

Despite difficulties in initial risk-taking of that kind, she does *not* think that men are more resistant against counselling, and often they are far more open-minded. 'Women tend more easily to feel that they have it all worked out and know it all,' she said. 'Men are more aware that they don't, and the experience of having someone else ask questions about aspects of themselves they haven't thought about can help them *not* to go down the old well-worn paths that some women tread.

'It is a matter of understanding the effects one's behaviour has on a partner and realising that sometimes the motivation behind it is not as kindly as we may like to think.'

That is why she considers marriage guidance a reflective process and not a crisis service. People who come for counselling as a last-ditch effort to save a crumbling edifice may not save their marriage but they can, if they are willing to take on board what is offered, come away with some deeper knowledge of themselves that will help in another relationship.

'Not everyone can use counselling,' she admits. 'Some want just a death certificate for the marriage or exoneration from blame and that isn't what we can provide. But most people do learn a lot and carry it into their lives.'

Because men traditionally have fewer close friends, fewer caring outsiders who can show them to themselves, they may benefit even more from counselling or therapy than women. Both sexes can derive the insights that ensue from talking to an impartial third party but, for more men, the process of unburdening themselves fully is itself a new and valuable experience. One man said to me that counselling had been '*the* most significant experience of my life'.

Practically, it isn't an easy option for very many people, however. Time off work for a man to go during the day may be hard to arrange on more than a short-term basis. There are, however, now a number of services designed to help in the short-term with the practical problems of divorce – who is going where, what happens to the children – which often become so destructively emotionally charged. Surveys show variously that between a quarter and over half of couples say nothing to their children about divorce until the separation has taken place. From the accounts given to me, feelings about how and when the children's emotions were handled remained strong even years after the event. Those who tried to hide the breakdown of the marriage from their children tended to regret it while those who were as honest and open as the ages of their children could allow recalled that aspect of the break-up as one they felt positive and grateful about.

It is over children, of course, that men and women's perspectives are most likely to diverge. A woman who has care of her children and whose divorce from her husband was particularly acrimonious may well wish that he need play no further part in her life at all, while knowing he is still important to the children. She may also be fearful that her children may prefer their father over her and be anxious as well as resentful over the time they spend with him and the withdrawal symptoms they manifest afterwards. As one man put it, his wife felt that his new relationship with their son must seem idyllic to the son. Confined as it was to weekends, it entailed treats and pleasure in each other's company unmarred by the normal home routine of homework and tickings off about dirtying clothes and leaving messes.

Yet, for most men I spoke to, they felt far from triumphant that they could appear the more 'special' parent. A number expressed the feeling of being unreal to their children, unable to involve themselves in their day-to-day problems, unable to exert real influence as a father and deprived of the daily routines and chores concerned with their upbringing. The special quality of the weekend-fathering role was as stressful to them as it appeared idyllic to their ex-wives. They feared, if only at first, that their children's love had become more tenuous and that, because it was more precious, unless they were loving and giving all of the time, they might lose it. They found it harder to feel comfortable about acting naturally, saying no or feeling irritable, than their wives would in their normal daily relationship with the children.

A number of studies show that children's reaction to the separation of their parents varies according to age, with the youngest the most confused and often self-blaming, six- to eight-year-olds experiencing intense grief and suppressed anger, nine- to twelve-year-olds more openly angry than fearful and adolescents most open in their anger and upset, although usually best able to cope if they have, by then, strong self-esteem. In all cases, those whose parents were honest with them and who showed they each still loved them, adjusted the most quickly. Relationships with both parents were important, however bitter the parents felt towards each other.

Yet statistics show that forty per cent of the parents who are not looking after the children, usually the father, lose touch with them. I was very moved by the two accounts I heard from fathers who had broken off all or most contact with their children. Neither had done so because they didn't care but because they cared very much. Both felt they had become the 'disruptive' element in their children's lives, especially as their ex-wives had remarried to men very prepared to take on the children as their own. Both worried constantly about the rightness of the decision and I wonder if their wives would have realised what it cost them to make it. Neither attempted to dissuade them for the children's sake and one actively discouraged contact.

Of the majority of men I spoke to who had retained very strong relationships with their children, a number were honest enough to be able to admit that, whatever pain the marriage breakdown had caused, they knew that they had forged stronger bonds with the children as a result of being weekend fathers. They were aware that they had been pushed by circumstances into re-evaluating the role they played in their children's lives and vice versa. Some said they gave more attention to them, took more responsibility for them and started to see them as individuals in their own right, instead of as integral parts of the family. That may say something about traditional marriage, where for many men the focus is on their role as provider rather than nurturer. One man, who had become a parent reluctantly, admitted that he only saw his son for himself after the marriage had ended. It is a shift in attitude which again may give rise to some resentment from ex-wives, if they feel that their husbands have only chosen to assert themselves in their children's lives once the point has been reached where they can't take the family for granted. They may even see it as an exercise in vying for a child's affections and envy the easy relationship. But, from the men I spoke to, it seemed that it was *because* they accepted that their influence as a live-in father was reduced that they could relax their expectations, and allow themselves to see and respond to their children as people separate from themselves: as a few described it, as 'friends'.

I deliberately sought out two men who had custody of their children, locating them through Gingerbread, an organisation for single parents. But I was surprised to find that three of the others had also had full-time care of their children at some point. I did find myself admiring them for the love and commitment they showed to their children's well-being. I did not see them as having more problems than single mothers, just different problems, and yet I know I looked upon them as special, as many other people do. Again, it says so much about expectations of what comes naturally to women and to men, which is not borne out when it comes to individuals, and the strength to go against such expectations.

Also with the strength to go against expectations, if of a different kind, were the men who found that it didn't work for them to see as much of their children as they had originally thought essential. One, particularly, who had wanted his children to stay every weekend, reached a point where he realised that he personally needed some time at weekends for himself, to re-establish a social life and open himself to finding another relationship. He felt he had to become happier in himself and more outward-looking towards his future, settling in the end for the arrangement his wife had originally wanted – seeing the children every other weekend and one night in every other week. If he couldn't be what he wanted, a full-time father, then he wanted the best of both imperfect worlds and openly admitted it.

He was also one who expressed the view that his children had adapted far more naturally to having their parents live separately than he had. He feared and expected psychological damage to have been done to them by such an emotional trauma, even though he couldn't see the evidence. Most men felt the same, whatever the circumstances of the separation, but I was struck by the philosophical attitude many had been able to take – that they could only do their best to make good, whatever guilt they felt or had felt once. As one pointed out, children can be damaged by seemingly stable marriages too and what counts is the quality of caring in the end.

None of the men I spoke to felt floored by the domestic responsibilities of being alone, even though a great many had been used to having their physical needs taken care of during marriage. They felt deeply disoriented and lonely in their bought flats or rented bedsitters or while camping uncomfortably for a while on other people's sofas but the mechanics of coping with basic needs, such as food, clean sheets or laundered suits, presumably paled into oblivion next to the huge emotional and physical upheaval. Some learned, in fact, as time lessened the despair and depression, that they were perfectly capable of caring for their own needs and that housekeeping would not be a subtle element of attraction in a search for a second wife. Managing alone, often for the first time in their lives, may help many men to separate out what really is important to them in a relationship.

As one man put it, whose wife had been used to ply him with comforts and exquisite meals, 'I don't care if my next marriage is not materially rich but it has got to be emotionally rich.' Sometimes, as Lillian Rubin has pointed out, women may use physical acts of providing care and comforts as their own way of hiding a fear of true intimacy. They appear to be giving and yet not in the way that leaves them most emotionally vulnerable –

giving of themselves. While within the marriage, neither partner may quite realise what is going on, especially if the woman also uses the caring role to make her husband feel guilty.

One man recalled his wife resenting the fact that she felt expected to be doing the cooking yet, when he said he felt no need for her to take that role on herself, she felt rejected. However much she disliked the role, it had deeper significance than just who put meals on the table.

While the physical and financial effects of separation were obviously more pronounced for men who had children, divorce was not without significant impact for childless men. The sense of personal failure and self-questioning was as strong, particularly if the marriage had lasted a long time.

It was the childless men who often said how powerful marriage as an institution is, its ritual and public nature unconsciously leading them and their wives to stay within it longer than was useful, yet with an acceptance or complacency that prevented change.

It didn't seem to me that any of the men blithely rushed off after separation and then divorce into the life of 'gay bachelors', in the original sense of that term. Quite a few eschewed relationships completely for a long time, while they tried to sort out the pieces of their shattered identities or sank into depression or drink. Of those who did quickly start up relationships with other women, what they were searching for varied from a need to fill the emotional void, a need to re-establish faith in their attraction and performance as sexual males or a desire to 'get back' at women. Only a few mentioned that they had been 'scrupulously honest' with partners, if what they were looking for was sexual reassurance. While those who were seeking to fill an emotional void without having established what led to the last one generally caused for all concerned. Some felt so reckless and self-destructive after losing their families that they didn't even care.

I was very aware that the particular men I spoke to all found it relatively easy to meet women in the first place, unless they were the ones who had care of the children. And that in itself goes far to explain why so many divorced women find it more difficult to meet men, as they are more usually the ones who are full-time mothers. As one man reflected, while he was looking to meet women, he never came across divorcees with children. But there are a growing number of women who take the deliberate decision to concentrate on careers and not get married early, so there are plenty of mature single women around. Older men, on whole, find it easier as well to attract younger women than older women do younger men.

Yet half of the men I interviewed were currently single and quite a number by choice. Most had embarked quite swiftly on substitute relationships which failed and now shied away from total commitment. It was marked that those who professed satisfaction with an independent way of life had busy, engrossing careers or jobs and tended to have the opportunity to meet new people through work or busy social lives. Some had established what they saw as comfortable sexual friendships with women who also professed to be loath to enter commitment, and admitted they would feel less contented otherwise. But I got the impression that, though many appeared to be satisfied with several more superficial relationships, part of them still wanted a relationship that could grow, but without requiring too much compromise.

As one said: 'Press the right buttons and I might find myself pitching in all over again.' But taking a decision not to compromise is a decision to close up and protect against hurt, which itself may militate against the success of any relationship pitched into.

Most others, however, felt very strongly that they did want a new relationship to which they could give commitment – more commitment rather than less than in their previous marriages. If they had identified the part that their own failure to communicate and express emotions had played, they were keen to behave very differently second time around. Several made the point that they and their wives talked about everything and tried not to hide away negative feelings. Yet there is also so much more to go wrong. Complicated relationships between children and parents and step-parents may have to be negotiated, as well as continuing practical involvement over the children with ex-husbands or wives. Coupled with that, surveys show that second-time married partners tend to be much more realistic about what they want and less likely to stick around so long if they don't get it. More second marriages than first ones end in divorce.

Only a few men mentioned to me significant difficulties over second wives and children or jealousy between first and second wives. Many were in a position where only they but not their ex-wives, or vice versa, had married again or where, by the time both re-married, the children were already almost adults. Yet some did mention a different difficulty, that of handling friendships with women made prior to second marriage or those with men that had been made by their wives. By the time couples embark on second marriage, they are far more likely than first-time rounders to have friends who are independent of each other and unknown quantities as far as the new partner is concerned. Some may be former lovers.

The solution will inevitably be an individual one. Some men said that they were prepared, or they expected to give up previous associations, perhaps because the relationships had been primarily sexual, whereas other men found that their new wives were unwilling to sever friendships with men whom they knew because the foundation of those relationships were not, or were no longer, sexual. The wives trusted the men and expected to be trusted likewise, but the men had to confront their feelings about jealousy and double standards, and also about how they viewed friendship. It could, of course, have been the other way around. I wouldn't dare speculate about whether men or women are more likely to be threatened by a partner's opposite sex friends but traditionally, at least, men are more likely to see each other as rivals. 'The selfish gene' is one controversial anthropological theory that attempts to explain this. We are, the theory goes, all driven to ensure the evolutionary survival of our genes, but males, by the fleeting nature of their reproductive role, can never be certain that they are fathers of their mate's offspring. Primitive instinct of most males of the species in the wild is to spread their own sperm widely while viewing as competitors any male who comes near the chosen females. On some primitive level, this theory would have us conclude, male jealousy has an extra dimension to that suffered by both sexes arising from general insecurity.

One man expressed to me the view that jealousy is inevitable in a long relationship, if it isn't one that survives on the safety of routine, where nothing threatening is looked at too closely. Psychologist Abraham Maslow wouldn't agree. Jealously is part of what he defined as D-love – deficiency love that is based on selfish need and which only survives as long as all needs are met. Whereas B-love is about being, an abandoned and total giving of one's whole self to another, without reserve. It is heady stuff indeed, as he describes it in *Toward a Psychology of Being*.

'Since it is non-possessive,' he wrote, 'and is admiring rather than needing, it makes no trouble and is practically always pleasure-giving. B-lovers are more independent of each other, more autonomous, less jealous or threatened, less needful, more individual . . . but simultaneously more eager to help the other toward self-actualisation, more proud of his (her) triumphs, more altruistic, generous, fostering. B-love . . . creates the partner. It gives him (her) a self-image, it gives him (her) a self-acceptance, a feeling of love-worthiness, all of which permit him (her) to grow.'

I imagine that it is only if two people could trust that their own needs *would* also be met that they could give of themselves so freely. The more secure each partner feels, the more they can offer both the nurturing and the space to let each other grow. For it is a risky business and many of us are more likely either to fear that we may lose part of ourselves in marriage or to embrace it as a way of avoiding facing ourselves and living instead through somebody else.

That makes me reflect on what the ritual of marriage itself actually means for either sex, any religious aspects apart. A number of men felt that, even though they wanted or had a committed relationship, they wouldn't marry again. Some others married because their partners wanted to feel secure, otherwise they would not have felt it necessary to legalise the alliance. But, as one man said, marriage doesn't guarantee security any more. In fact it means quite the opposite. It means risk. It means letting go  of at least the image of emotional independence which living together may more comfortably provide. Buying property together, even having children together, are often seen as less committing, in some strange portion of the psyche, than the actual act of marriage, despite protestations about the outmodedness of or lack of necessity for the ritual.

The same need to bolster or protect our sense of identity may lead one person to embrace marriage and another to eschew it. But if we *need* to be married or we need *not* to be married to a live-in partner, perhaps the question of total commitment, and therefore the depth of giving and receiving that with courage could be possible, has been skirted.

There is no doubt much more that could be said but these are thoughts inspired by what I heard from the particular men I spoke to. And what they said confirmed for me that very old adage – marriage has to be worked at if we want it to last and stay alive. If it takes the sad experience of marriage breakdown and divorce to reveal that, it is a powerful learning process indeed. It may have been the nature of the men who were willing to speak to me but all for whom the trauma was a few years in the past felt more confident and positive about themselves now, whatever road they had chosen to tread, and even if guilt or battles or pain over children's lives persisted.

It was interesting to me that two men chose the same simile to evoke the experience of marriage breakdown and divorce. They described it as like a first parachute jump – a paralysingly terrifying experience, its outcome unknown – and they had survived it. So had the rest. Whatever they wished they had or had not done, learned earlier or acted on sooner, they were once more able to feel positive about a strong part of themselves and the future. Whatever sadness they sustained for pain caused and suffered, they had also found happiness or hope.